ACCLAIM FOR *THE EPIC CLASSROOM*

"I hope that every teacher reads this essential book and brings the ideas inside it to the classroom. And it would help if every parent bought a copy and sent it in to school with their kids."

Seth Godin
Author of *Stop Stealing Dreams*

"Want to learn how to create 'epic' projects that take your students on heroes' journeys? Trevor Muir's clear and engaging book offers a step-by-step process for transforming your classroom to a place where academic content standards, skills, and intrinsic motivation all come together in compelling ways. A must-read for anyone who aspires to really teach."

Tony Wagner
Harvard I-Lab Expert in Residence
Author of *The Global Achievement Gap* and *Creating Innovators*

"If you want to take student engagement in your classroom to the next level, this is the book for you. A blueprint to bring stories into your classroom no matter what you teach or for how long."

David Prindle
President of MACUL

"Trevor has been a forced to be reckoned with online. After reading *The Epic Classroom*, I have even a deeper appreciation for his creativity and wisdom. This book challenged my thinking and left me with a fire re-lit inside. I was encouraged and pushed throughout my time reading this book. I would definitely recommend this to anyone in education."

Todd Nesloney
Prominent Speaker, Principal, and
Author of *Kids Deserve It*

"In *The Epic Classroom,* Muir takes us on a journey through the possibilities of what great teaching and memorable learning can be. The suggestions are practical and flexible. The stories are moving and tie the ideas to who we are at our best as we teach. This is a book for teachers who want to see something more powerfully memorable in their work, and who believe that the teacher's power to change lives is not platitude, but the joy and reward that comes from having the courage to be a professional educator."

Rushton Hurley
Author of *Making Your School Something Special*

THE EPIC CLASSROOM

How to Boost Engagement,
Make Learning Memorable,
and Transform Lives

TREVOR MUIR

BLEND EDUCATION
Salem, Oregon
2017

BLEND

Blend Education

PO Box 5953

Salem, OR 97304

www.blendeducationpublishing.com

The Epic Classroom: How to Boost Engagement, Make Learning Memorable, and Transform Lives / Trevor Muir. -- 1st ed.

ISBN-13: 978-0692910924 (Blend Education)
ISBN-10: 0692910921

Dedication

*To Honey Nun, for showing me that epic
learning never ends.*

ACKNOWLEDGMENTS

I'd like to express my gratitude to my publisher, Blend Education, for believing in *The Epic Classroom* before a word was written. Especially John Spencer- thanks for your guidance, honesty, wisdom, expertise, and conversation as we made this dream a reality.

Thanks to the Andersons for investing in my crazy aspirations.

I am forever grateful to Aaron Carrier for teaching me the foundation of what stories are, and why they are so powerful.

Thank you to the administrators at Byron Center High School for letting me stand on tables, blast rap music in the hallways, and make learning epic.

I'm grateful for Devon Bailey who took the time to read through the first draft and help me realize the fine art of using the delete button.

Thanks to my whole family, who are some of the most inspiring people on the face of the earth. Especially my mama, who had me writing books as soon as I could walk.

Thank you, Jack and Marcia for never ceasing to believe in your kids' greatness, and doing everything you can to support it.

All my love for my beautiful kids, Jack and Piper. The fire and zest for life you have is exactly why school needs to be epic. What a crime it would be if you ever lost it.

And special thanks to my wife, Alli, for all of the work you put into this book too. Being with the kids while I worked, dealing with my frustration, giving honest feedback, and being a ceaseless source of encouragement and inspiration. You are wonderful.

CONTENTS

"Every revolution begins with a spark"

THE BONFIRE

W HEN I WAS TWELVE, my buddies and I went camping. We were four smelly preteens sitting around a roaring bonfire telling stories, roasting marshmallows, talking about girls.

Pure freedom from parents, technology, and the world as we celebrated the fleeting moments of childhood and the impending privileges that come with age.

As the night waned and the excessive levels of caffeine began to wear off, it was time to retire to our tents. It was my job to put the fire out, and so before bed I poured a bucket of water on it and spread out the coals.

But the next day, when we climbed out of our tents, there was still smoke coming from where the fire was.

Not flames, but a few embers that somehow survived being smashed apart by a stick, a bucket of water, and a long quiet night.

Luckily, I didn't burn down the forest. My friends gave me one of those brief, "you could have killed us," stares, and I proceeded to collect sticks and twigs to build a new fire using the surviving embers from the night before.

My son is a toddler who sees the world in bright and bursting colors. Everything is an adventure to him. Life is a story and he is the hero who defeats dragons, creates works of art, and wants to know how the universe works. I don't have to make him want to learn; to him the world is fascinating. Life burns bright through the eyes of a three-year-old.

He is a bonfire.

But then toddlers get older and go to school, and their busy feet are hidden under desks, and the loud ones are called trouble-makers. Creating art is limited to an hour a day, or in some places, is considered a complete waste of time. It's a world where you primarily only learn letters and numbers to receive letters and numbers.

The letter A is used to illuminate wrong from right, ignoring hearts and shining bright on the left sides of brains to identify who is smart and who lacks the intelligence to get a score close to 100.

Don't get me wrong, some kids are motivated by those letters and numbers, or at least by the parents and teachers who expect the numbers to be high and the letters to be at the beginning of the alphabet.

But many, *many* students spend the vast majority of their childhoods in a desk watching the second hand on a clock slowly makes its way around enough times until a factory bell releases them to go home and sit quietly some more, and do more work, to get more *letters and numbers.*

Suddenly learning is not out of fascination, but obligation. Too many students are disengaged and memorizing instead of learning. Going through the motions to make their teachers and parents happy- or, to get the grades.

And is that learning?

If a student is not engaged, or even bored the vast majority of their time, is there really any chance of knowledge to be retained?

This is an issue that faces millions of young people in thousands of schools. The system entrusted to prepare people to become bright, intelligent, contributing, courageous, strong citizens has been hijacked by irrelevancy and practices that devalue the power of learning.

For too many people, school has become a bucket of water and a long quiet night.

Is there a better way to do school, one driven by engagement and real, authentic learning? And can teachers reclaim what it means to be in the classroom?

I think so.

Because I believe school can be a story, an epic adventure where students are heroes and their teachers enter the stories with them.

Classrooms can be a space, a setting, for creativity to flourish, lives to transform, and fires to ignite.

The education system needs work. But educators can reclaim this space. Enough water and idleness can put a campfire out. But sometimes there are still embers, and that fire can burn again.

"*People think that stories are shaped by people. In fact, it's the other way around.*"
                                                    -Terry Pratchett

CHAPTER 1

THE POWER
OF STORY

NINETY-THREE-YEAR-OLD hands grasp the palms of fourteen-year-old high school students as a group of seniors make their way off a bus and into a movie theater. Some of these same wrinkled hands held M1 carbine rifles on the day the U.S. invaded Normandy.

One set of hands held a poultice on the stomach of a dying best friend at the Battle of the Bulge. And another pair shook with relief as they held a newspaper that read that the war was finally over.

Now these World War II veterans are holding the hands of teenagers over seventy years later. These teenagers interviewed the veterans a month earlier, and filmed the experience with cell phones and cheap video cameras. They used free online editing software to turn the footage into documentaries that will premiere at this old theater, and give the veterans and their families a way to preserve their stories forever. This red-carpet event was originally conceived simply as a place for the students to showcase their work at the end of a history project.

But then the news found out about it.

And over 400 community members crowded into the small theater. When the veterans ambled into the auditorium behind walkers and in wheelchairs, the crowd roared so loud that people claimed to have heard the applause from the streets. A man with a bent back leaning over a walker stood a little taller as he walked down that red carpet. For two hours, people laughed, cried, and cheered as they watched 6-minute films bring the stories of these veterans to life. Films made by a group of high school students.

One man said that in the seventy years since he's been home from the war, he had never once been thanked for his service, and that this was one of the best nights of his life.

This man was no longer a number. In the eyes of 124 public high school students, he was a hero, and his story will not die with him.

And this was no longer just a history project.

Because instead of learning about World War II from lectures and textbooks, these students learned about it from him. Someone who was there; a primary source who breathed the air of the time and lived the stories.

Now this is history class.

What do you think the chances are that the students will ever forget this experience? These kids were motivated to learn and work by something way more profound than grades, parents, and even me, their teacher. They were motivated by capturing and telling the stories of World War II veterans, and getting to share these stories with the world.

When I was in high school, I learned about World War II from pages 269-298 in Prentice Hall's student edition of *Modern World History*. It told me that D-Day occurred on June 6th, 1944, in Normandy, France. I read that this was the Allied Force's first foothold in Europe during the war. The book taught that 9000 Allied soldiers died in the attack, but 100,000 were able to land on the beaches of France using Higgins Boats at the end of the battle.

I read the chapter twice and memorized every fact that I needed to remember. When it came time to answer the study questions at the end of the textbook chapter, I got every one of them correct. And on the test, I scored an easy A.

Fifteen years later, I remember *none* of it. This information is no longer living at the front of my brain. As a matter of fact, I discarded most of it when I got my test score back, and knew I would not retake the test. The knowledge I gained from the textbook and lectures was useless to me, and I'd much rather use my mental capacity at that time to remember more critical things, like all the dance moves to *Hammer Time*, or how to beat *Zelda*. I did not care to remember the dates and details of a war that was long over and did not relate to the miniscule bubble I lived in.

This content was not important to me.

Here's the thing though, the World War II content that I was presented with in high school is every bit as compelling as the content my students are learning today. The stories of heroism and valor could be found within my history teacher's state standards, and even hidden in places on that ancient textbook. But they were not presented to me in a way that I could retain them. They were instead facts and information about people and places that had nothing to do with me.

My body and mind were not engaged, and a disengaged student retains very little that you teach them. They might remember it for a time, but that information is stored on the short-term memory shelves of one's brain. It is temporary. Inconsequential. And it occurs far too often in classrooms.

The question has to be asked, was a huge portion of my childhood – the thousands and thousands of hours spent hearing and seeing information that I would not retain, and thousands of more hours not paying attention to it, thus not learning anything in the first place- a complete waste?

Of course, there were valuable experiences weaved into my time in school, and I learned many skills that I still use today (I'm using some of them to write this book right now), but what could I have gained if the sum of many of those hours was not boredom and minor growth? What if the valuable learning experiences were not just sprinkled into my time in school, but were the fabric and bedrock of mandatory education? What could our students gain if school addressed this issue of disengaging and forgettable learning experiences?

Disengaging

Do you remember the buzz in the air the day you walked into biology class and knew that that was the day you'd get to dissect a frog?

I can't tell if you're nodding your head yes or not. This might've been a ninth-grade-boy-thing.

If you were anything like me in the ninth grade, that class period was special. Our teacher told us to make sure we brought our textbooks that day, because on page 325 was a diagram of a frog's anatomy, and we would need it to know where to cut, splice, and dissect – three things I didn't usually do in biology class. In fact, almost every other day was spent listening to lectures and taking notes.

But this class period allowed students to work with their hands and explore the unknown world of the anatomy of a dead amphibian. The textbook diagram came to life, and hearts were no longer just metaphors for the place love is stored, but instead muscle tissue that you can feel and see. On this day, the students were no longer just students, they were scientists.

Surely my teacher saw how engaged her room was that day, including the ninth-grade boy who normally could not sit still for an hour. Her lesson inspired students to engage in the moment and form lasting memories of the learning experience.

And yet, the next day of that class was back to lectures, textbooks, and worksheets; a room full of disengaged students. An engaging classroom does not need to be a rare experience, but too often it is.

Forgettable

A lecture on ancient civilizations, a slideshow about putting poetry into stanzas, or a worksheet on long division is almost always forgettable. The information may be usable for a time, but most 40-year-old adults will not be able to explain iambic pentameter to you or divide 3987 by 13. This isn't to say that either of these skills are not worthwhile, but the method in which they are often taught in schools is not effective in creating lasting knowledge. Learning needs to be sticky; certain methods and formats can be applied to the content that you already have mastered, and make the teaching of that subject matter last in the minds and bodies of learners.

I once labored for many hours creating a slideshow to teach my students the primary causes for the Cold War. This was a relevant issue found in my content standards that I believed was critical for them to understand modern conflicts and issues. I've always favored interactive lessons and projects, but for this subject I made a point to stick solely to direct instruction. I lectured for an entire class period with this slideshow and gave students an extensive outline for them to take notes with. I had a pop quiz the day after the lecture, where I made sure students refreshed themselves with the information, and had them create notecards with the information to study for the exam at the end of the unit.

And then on exam day, nearly 100% of my students aced the portion of the test about the causes of the Cold War. I was elated, and felt I learned something valuable about effective teaching through this experience.

The following fall, the history teacher for the grade level above mine came into my room during planning period and asked me why I did not cover the Cold War the year before. He said he gave a short formative assessment on that subject and nearly every student failed it. He talked with them afterwards, and they all said that they did not remember learning about it, or if they did, they did not remember the specifics.

So, either summer vacation sucked the knowledge out of their brains, or I wasn't as great of a teacher as I thought.

The teaching that I did for that unit was advantageous for the test that I gave, but honestly not for anything else. I'm sure students and parents were happy to see A's on the report cards, but otherwise the learning was valueless. If learning is not memorable, is it still successful?

Neural Coupling

A group of professors at Princeton University did a study on a recently discovered phenomenon called neural coupling[1]. They found that when a story is well told, the listener's brain is actually firing in almost the exact same patterns and in the same locations as the storyteller's brain did when the actual story occurred. The listener's brain is essentially mirroring the brain of the speaker, and cannot even distinguish between recalling memories of an experience and hearing it for the first time. They consciously know the story did not happen to them, but at a neurological level they do not.

If I told you about a time I went shark fishing with my buddies in high school, and described being in the middle of a harbor on a 15 foot boat, and that the smell of salt was so thick in the air that you could taste it; then black thunder clouds seemed to appear in the bright blue sky; and I told you how the engine would not start as we tried to escape the oncoming storm, and so we had to sit in the middle of a giant bay as lightning hit the water around us as we frantically bailed the warm saltwater that tried to sink the small boat that was keeping three high school students alive; and if my voice rose louder when I told you about the point of true desperation, when we considered that we might not make it back to shore, and three tough boys let themselves cry in front of each other as we believed we were breathing our last breaths, and at the pinnacle of our despair one of us tried the engine one last time, only to hear it fire up; and three fourteen-year-old boys howled with the wind as we sped to shore- your brain would not know that you were not in the boat with me and my two friends. The story would physically imprint the experience in your brain in the same way that the experience imprinted in mine when I was fourteen.

When you heard about the smell of salt water, the part of your brain that processes smell would be at work. As you heard about the dark clouds and waves crashing over the sides of the boat, your brain would be creating images of that scene and mirror the patterns of my brain when it happened.

When you listened to the tale of three boys reduced to tears because of powerful forces of nature, your brain processed that emotion and imagined what it would be like to be in that situation. In fact, during the stressful moments of the story your brain would release cortisol, a hormone your body releases when stressed, designed to help you focus during stressful situations. The happy ending of the story releases dopamine, which triggers hope and optimism. It's why commercials can make you cry and horror movies are so hard to look away from.

This is the mysterious power of a well-told story.

The Princeton study even found that the greater anticipation or suspense within the story, the stronger the coupling or mirroring that occurs. When one of the veterans described the cold chill of the air over the English Channel on the morning of D-Day, my students' brains processed that information as if they at one time were in that Higgins Boat right alongside him.

It's why my students now have a much stronger grasp on World War II than I ever did. They were a part of it, a part of history in a very real and unique way.

Their experience with this veteran taught my students more about World War II than any textbook ever could. And I think that is because this war was no longer a black and white picture to them, or a list of facts and dates on a timeline. Instead this piece of history lived and breathed, full of gruesome pain and torment, but also a unique beauty that was woven into this story.

Stories animate what was lifeless.

There is a reason Homer's *Odyssey* has lived in color and sound in human's minds for almost three thousand years. Hearing about a person who embarked on an adventure full of pain and beauty is something that reso-nates with all of us. We can relate to that, and this theme is at the heart of any good story.

It's more than just telling what happened. It's paint-ing the three-act structure in someone else's mind, giving images to the beginning, middle, and end of a tale. Stories have the power to move and shape us. It is in our biology, our chemistry as human beings to react in such a profound way to one another when we hear tales of adventure, sadness, joy, etc.

It explains why humans went thousands of years with solely an oral tradition, passing on history and her-itage to each generation with stories. It's why millions of kids disappeared for three days each time a new *Harry Potter* book was released.

Stories are foundational to who we are as people and are at the very core of growth and development. They are why you remember very little from slideshows that contain nothing but graphs and data, but can quote eve-ry word from *Forrest Gump*. Information presented in story does not just make a brief appearance on the brain and then evaporate once that information was used. In-stead, it physically and permanently sears itself to your mind, ready to be accessed and used at any moment.

There is more to stories than simple entertainment. Story has immense power.

And yet our education system, which has the primary purpose of growing and developing people into intelligent, contributing, well-rounded human beings-has largely lost sight of this integral medium of teaching. Rote memorization and a blanketed standardization of knowledge has become the dominant method of educating children.

In the early twentieth century, America was at the height of the Industrial Era. The population was booming, and enormous factories were built to mass produce food and manufactured goods for the rapidly growing society. America needed a system that could prepare a workforce of millions of people to work these factories and turn the nation into an economic superpower.

Our current model of education emerged in this context.

A system was designed to turn children into optimal factory workers. They learned how to obey orders because rule following was key to efficient factories. Kids sat at desks lined up in rows to simulate standing in rows on assembly lines. Loud metal bells released students from class, triggering their time to transition to another task in the same way factory bells were utilized. School was made to be 8 hours long, the same amount of time as a factory workday.

This system was very successful. For over a century, America did have a booming factory-dominated economy with workers who needed little on-site training and preparation to work their lives in factories and make the United States the richest country in the world. School served its purpose. Those who excelled in it were given additional attention leading to a white-collar career, while the majority went on to work in manufacturing.

However, here is the problem: in 2016, only nine percent of jobs in America are in manufacturing[2], and a growing majority of those jobs do not entail assembly line work and unskilled labor. At an increasing rate, workers are no longer standing in lines, hearing bells, or receiving direct instruction from their supervisors.

But school still does all of these things. It emulates a world that has since evolved.

The economic landscape has changed, the way businesses look has changed, America has changed- but school has not.

This outdated system that does not reflect the 21st century creates a lack of engagement in students. They are aware that much of it is about grades, test scores, and achieving enough to move to the next grade level. No matter how incredible many teachers are, and there are a lot fantastic teachers, if the framework they are working in is not engaging, students will not be engaged. School needs value, a purpose beyond achieving test scores so pupils can move to the next level in the system.

Now this is not to make the case that there is not a place for grades, tests, and even content in schools. This is not a "blow-up -the-system" book, trying to devise an entirely new framework for education. Without question, there are fantastic, meaningful, and effective practices happening in traditional classrooms all over the place. However, if the emphasis of a student's time in school is solely to gain content knowledge and pass tests, strong teaching methods will not compensate for a system that is based on a purpose that students do not connect with. Students need to form deep connections with what they are learning, interacting with content in a way that creates permanence.

Epic Learning

As teachers and educators, we have already mastered the content that we want our students to learn and retain. So, the task of an effective teacher is how to deliver that content in a way that engages. I would argue that any content from any subject area can be crafted into a story. There is an art to making lectures into stories, and this book will address how to do that.

But the bulk of this book goes beyond direct instruction and delivery of information from teachers to students. Instead, it is about crafting your classroom, your units, and projects, lessons into actual stories.

Beyond just telling stories in class, students can be a part them. Lesson plans and curriculum can be crafted in the shape of a narrative, and presented in a way that neural coupling can occur as students interact within a story in your classroom. Whether students know that they are interacting in an ongoing, intentional story is irrelevant. When they are presented with a conflict they have to solve, developing as characters, existing in a setting crafted for a specific purpose, being exposed to themes much more significant than grades, and seeing something through to its resolution- a lasting imprint is made on their minds and souls.

Project-Based Learning is an instructional method that heightens engagement by giving students practical and authentic purpose to the work they do in the classroom. At the heart of a project based learning classroom are the projects and having significant and meaningful lessons tied into the learning. Epic learning takes the engaging concept of project-based learning, but delivers it in a way that the skills, content, and experience are imprinted in student's minds because the project was shaped into a narrative. Students and teachers work within a narrative and are part of an unfolding story. The connections created by authenticity are made deeper and lasting because story is at the center of the learning experience.

This book is about how to structure classes and projects into epics. Each chapter will describe a different part of the process to create and put epic learning in your classroom. Whether teaching history, language arts, science, or math; kindergartners to high school seniors- any subject in any grade level can be presented in this captivating way. Instead of delivering knowledge that will be processed and regurgitated, class can be a space where students are characters in a plot. A plot with conflict, climaxes, and resolve.

Suspenseful curriculum.

Compelling lesson plans.

A place containing failure and success. There are protagonists and antagonists in the material we want students to learn (my antagonist is trigonometry). Themes and structure that students can identify; creating an abiding change on their hearts and minds.

This is epic learning.

When we deliver school like a story to be experienced, knowledge is not just memorized; it is learned. It is housed in the minds of students in a remarkable and permanent way. Like the particulars of a fishing trip, the details of a formula, or a historic event- experiences are imprinted in the minds of learners.

Learning is no longer defined by rigor; instead by engagement. Whether huge and dynamic projects that burst beyond the walls of your school building, or small intimate ones where students quietly learn who they are, this learning serves to transform students forever. It is memorable and powerful.

It is *an* epic.

And it is epic.

"Give the story chemistry"

CHAPTER 2

THE FIVE
ELEMENTS

B EFORE WE START BREAKING down epic learning and how to set your class up in this way, I'm going to tell you about a project and describe the key elements of epic learning within it. The following chapters will go into more detail for each of these elements, and describe how you can do epic learning yourself. Once you understand what these elements are, and how they can be woven into curriculum and projects, it's just a matter of planning them out and letting the story begin.

Unless you are an English teacher, you may not have heard about the different elements of a story since you were thirteen and copied them on the back of your hand before a test. So, let's refresh.

A complete story – one that fully engages the mind of readers, listeners and participants –includes five elements. The presence of these elements is what gives a story purpose and value. If one of them is missing from a story, it is not really a story.

If a friend said to you, *"I have got to tell you the story of my trip to the grocery store!*

I walked down the aisle, picked up some bananas and cereal, and after paying for them, I got in my car and drove home. Great story, right!"

You would probably ask,

"And then what?"

They reply, *"Nothing, that's all that happened. Wasn't it amazing?"*

"No. That is the worst story ever. It was worse than 50 Shades of Grey and Twilight combined. I will never get those 20 precious seconds of my life back. I am now worse because of it.

Harsh.

That was such a weak story because it wasn't a story at all. It was missing the key elements that create engagement. Strong neural coupling is reliant on all of the elements of a story being present. Otherwise it is just information, and unless it is presented in a compelling way, it often does not stick. The same can be said for successful engagement in your classroom.

Here is a brief summary of each of the elements of a story. Try to begin framing these elements as you might see them in your classroom, figuring out where they might fit in.

The Elements of a Story

Theme

The theme is the central idea or belief in a story. Some stories might have multiple themes, others just one dominant theme that the narrative focuses on. You can also think of themes as underlying lessons for the characters to learn. Some examples of themes in stories would be bravery, power, or coming-of-age.

Plot

A plot is a series of events and actions that devise or present the sequence of a story. It is the road on which all of the other elements live, and make a story more than just gathered information. The plot is what moves the information along and binds it together.

Every plot should have a story arch, a defined *beginning, middle,* and *end.* This is where the action takes place, and lets the reader, listener, or student understand the motion and progress of the narrative.

Setting

The setting of a story is the time and place in which the story happens. It is where the story takes place, and has a major effect on how it unfolds. Setting influences who characters are and how they act in their world.

Characters

The characters are the people, or sometimes animals and objects (think *Toy Story*) that take part in the action of a story. They are the ones getting their hands dirty and making their way through the plot. Characters shape and develop as a plot progresses, evolving along with the story. Main characters very rarely make it to the end of a tale unchanged.

Conflict

The conflict is the problem in the story that needs to be solved. There is no such thing as a story without conflict, otherwise it is just information. Conflict is crucial for giving the story a purpose, and without it, you just have a bunch characters existing in a setting without any plot moving them forward and thereby not learning and growing and developing themes from their experiences. Without any type of conflict, boredom sets in. Have you ever arrived at an exotic tropical vacation spot, and thought, "I will never get sick of this? I could lay in this hammock staring at the beach forever."

And then two weeks later you were bored.

Not because the setting was any less beautiful, or the people you are with are any less interesting, but because there was nothing challenging you. Sitting idle with nothing to activate your brain is great sometimes. We need rest and breaks from life's conflicts. But epic stories rarely happen in rest, and that's why vacations should not last forever.

Or at least that's what I think. I'm kind of weird though.

Now you know the five elements of a story. Remember them, because there will be a test later (not really). I am going to describe a project from a project based, epic learning environment, and identify where the elements of a story were woven into the project. Again, we will go into detail on planning and implementing each of these later on.

When learning about the Industrial Revolution, I wanted my class of high school freshmen to understand the concept of modernity. Modernity is a term that describes the rapid social and technological growth humans experience at different stages in history. For instance, Julius Caesar and George Washington, men who lived almost 2000 years apart from each other, had the same mode of transportation to get around in their days: riding on the backs of big hairy mammals. Transportation was primitive and changed very little over that huge span of time. But then, about 150 years after George Washington's lifetime, humans could travel 20 thousand miles per hour and land a vehicle on the moon. That's a rapid and major advancement in transportation technology, and one of the many enormous leaps humans made during this Revolution.

This is modernity, and it is a **theme** gleaned from my state content standards about industrialism. The modernity happening before our very eyes is astounding. From the internet, cellular technology, medical advances, or social changes, modernity is a dominant theme in our modern society.

Once I have identified a theme that I want the project to focus on, I can start to brainstorm how my students can be a part of a story that will help them understand it. Because if they have understanding of the major themes within this project, the rest of the content knowledge will follow. The theme helps bring focus to everything else.

Then I move on to thinking about the **setting** for the project. Where can this project take place for the characters to learn and grow? What is class going to look like for the next month or so? What is going to be the authentic environment my students will work in? This is still brainstorming, and I'm trying to envision the world the story will take place.

Now that I've located a theme in the content standards and have attempted to answer broad questions about the potential setting, I have to think of how to tie it all together and come up with a project for my students. At the time I designed this project, I was also learning about refugees and the plight many make in escaping their home countries because of natural disasters and war. Because this was an issue I was becoming passionate about, I wanted my students to share that interest as well. The theme from these specific content standards provided that opportunity. Here is how I made the connection:

Refugees are people who have been displaced from their homes because of human-caused and environmental disasters. Countries like the United States give refuge or safe haven to thousands of refugees every year. Quite often, refugees come from countries that have not yet experienced the technological modernity that America has experienced. Their countries were not directly a part of the Industrial Revolution that took place the last three hundred years. However, when they step off of an airplane into US cities, it is almost as if these refugees from less-developed countries are experiencing their own Industrial Revolution in a matter of minutes rather than decades and centuries.

As I was thinking about the theme and setting for this project, I made this connection between refugees and my content standards. Through a process I will describe later in this book, I began to develop a project idea of having my students learn about the struggles of incoming refugees to the United States while simultaneously learning about the Industrial Revolution.

I called a local social work agency and asked if they knew of any refugees who would be willing to come to my class and share their story. At this point in the planning process, I didn't yet know exactly what my students could do to assist refugees or even what the specific conflict of our story would be. I did know I wanted them to engage in serving people and create something that would be of actual use. The foundation of the project was there, but not the specifics. However, I felt that the students hearing from an actual person who has been on the journey of a refugee would be a worthy experience, and might produce a concrete project idea.

I was right.

On a Monday morning at 7:00 a.m., a woman named Danysa came and spoke to my class. She talked about losing her entire family to violence twenty years ago in the Rwandan genocide. Danysa talked to my students about her husband being killed with a machete as she hid inside a hotel room at the *Hotel des Mille Collines*. You might have seen the movie. I did not have to tell any students in my class to put their cell phones away that morning. The room was silent, and all eyes were glued to the front of the room where a Rwandan woman used broken English to share her story.

Danysa fled to a refugee camp in Kenya where she lived for over a decade on nothing more than rice and corn. And then one day, she was put on an airplane and without the slightest clue to where it was going, ended up in Grand Rapids, Michigan. She landed in January, and had never heard of snow before. She said the first time that it snowed, she thought that there was a volcano nearby, and that it was strange, cold ash falling from the sky. Danysa shared how she did not speak English, did not know how to use a light switch, had never seen a toilet in person, did not know what to eat. She knew no one and did not have any friends. She once got on a city bus and did not know how to signal that she needed to get off, and so stayed on that bus all day until the driver reached the end of his route and made Danysa get off- in January- during a snowstorm.

My students could not believe what they were hearing. In the isolated world that many of them live in, the idea of this kind of thing happening in America was absolutely foreign. Finding out that it was happening in their own neighborhoods was heartbreaking.

This story officially had a **conflict**. A very real problem that needed to be solved.

When Danysa left that morning, my students talked with each other, and decided that there has to be a way to help refugees avoid some of the problems they face when coming to America. One of my outspoken students yelled out, "This is stupid. How come no one showed her how to stop a bus? It's not that hard."

Yes, opinionated student, it is stupid that no one showed them that. Maybe you can.

Next, I directed an inquiry process that led students to coming up with the idea to create tools that would help refugees better assimilate into modern society. We weren't sure what these tools would look like, and I was not sure exactly what they'd create when I conceptualized the project, but a basic idea was formed, and the students owned it.

They heard and were moved by Danysa's story. The students learned that Danysa is not alone in this struggle, and that they could serve a role in solving this con-flict that they were presented with.

And so, for the next month, my classroom **setting** changed. It was no longer just a place where English and History content was delivered.

It was a social work agency.

Students were on their phones daily talking with ref-ugees around the area, learning their needs and brainstorming how to solve those needs. One group was in contact with a translator who translated all of the English my students wrote on "How to Use Appliances" flashcards, to Swahili. Kids were filming how-to videos, they were creating cookbooks, using Photoshop to de-sign brochures; designing and creating products that would make a quantifiable difference in the world.

If you were an outsider and walked into my class-room at any given time during this project, you would see a workplace environment full of impassioned and determined workers. Kids driven by the idea of serving and acting outside of themselves. The students were **characters** in a story about giving, hope, design, and hard work.

I called the same social work agency I contacted ear-lier, and told them about what my students were working on, and asked if they would be interested in coming to my classroom and allowing my students to present their final products to them. If they liked any of the products that they saw, or felt any of them could have use in their program, they could take the tools back with them. The agency of course said yes. Because a large group of talented and energetic students were offering free tools and resources to them, and were in the early stages of becoming advocates for refugees. So, at the end of this unit, the class presented these tools.

The students put on their best outfits because they knew it was not a normal presentation; they were presenting to working professionals. The social workers sat in my classroom, joined by some other refugees who came to provide some firsthand knowledge, and my students began presenting their work. Group after group, students made their way to the front of the room to show their fine-tuned products to our guests. My students acted like seasoned professionals themselves that day, and were more focused, serious, and engaged than I'd ever seen them before.

This was the climax of the story. Everything leading to this day and moment was a part of a partially designed, but also uncharted **plot** full of challenge and adventure.

And now if you go into the waiting room at the social work agency we worked with, you will see flashcards typed in Swahili and Arabic on how to use household appliances sitting on a coffee table in the waiting room. A how-to video created by a group of fourteen-year-olds about how to use the public transportation system is playing on loop in that lobby. And in a side room every week there is a group of teenage refugees that meets, and at the first of these meetings they play a video about making friends in America.

This is a story students will remember. It contains all of the elements that activate the brain and inspire authentic engagement. It was epic in another way, as the task was grand and the climax was huge. Sometimes that alone has the power to captivate students.

As a teacher for this class, my first task is to conceptualize and plan a project that has all 5 elements of a story woven into it. My next task is making sure I utilize this engagement to its full potential. This means I am facilitating conversations about refugees, talking about product development, emphasizing collaboration and accountability, and teaching other important skills students need to develop in school.

There can be a lot of moving parts to a project like this, and sometimes at the end of the school day I ask myself why I didn't just order some textbooks and talk for 45 minutes- that seems way easier. But then I reflect on the characters in this story, and how they are growing and being stretched in ways school hasn't traditionally done. I also think about how I grow through these challenges, and how much more engaged I am in a project like this.

I also utilize this engagement in their development of content knowledge. When I'm wearing my history-hat during this project, I design lessons and instruction around tying what we are learning about modernity with refugees to modernity in the Industrial Revolution. This historical content that can be found within my state standards makes much more sense when it is tied to what they are already doing and interacting with.

When I am in English-teacher-mode (And I am always in English teacher mode. This is why Twitter can drive me nuts), having a group of students who are excited and engaged in what they are doing on the project, then write a paper about it, is not that painful. The positive emotions generated by working on something authentic and using both sides of the brain carries over to most aspects of the classroom, including the content that is usually deemed as boring and pointless.

The class determined early on in this project that understanding the theme of modernity is vital, and that we would need to be able to grasp it to better serve our clients- the refugees. Therefore, an expository essay about the meaning of modernity and what it has looked like in history makes sense.

Now did I find a creative way to relate MLA format to the project and get students to understand its importance through the lens of story?

No. Few people ever have.

But by the time we got to MLA format, the project had won the students over. Being a part of Danysa's story engaged the learners; activated their minds. Pouring some of that excitement and energy into formatting was an easy task for most students.

And that is because the content is no longer boring and pointless.

This is why epic learning has a place in any content area. If an algebra class can tell a story in their work, one where all five of the elements are in play, the content makes sense. Math can make sense. Science can make sense. School can make sense if it is purposeful, and I will say it again, engaging.

The trick is, you just have to know how to do it. The rest of this book will look at how to plan an epic project and unit, then how to put the project in action, and finally how to process everything that happened in the story once it is over.

This all requires some paradigm shifting; moving away from comfortable lesson planning where the teacher can anticipate having total control of the learning process, and instead giving that process up to an unfolding story. Making this leap requires time and patience, but above all, creativity. Sir Ken Robinson, the famous TED education speaker who apparently rides around on a white steed (get it, because he's a knight), once said: "Teaching is a creative profession."[3]

We are not robots. Or walking textbooks.

Or playback machines that regurgitate information to other machines whose job it is to write down that information and remember it for a short time.

Instead we are creatives.

And with a little direction on how to create and execute class as a story, you can be a part of creating experiences for students that will not just evaporate after a test or a semester. You can help craft stories that live in the minds and lives of students long after they leave the walls of your classroom and school.

So, let's embark and get this adventure rolling.

We must go beyond textbooks; go out into the bypaths and untrodden depths of the wilderness and travel and explore and tell the world the glories of our journey.
                         -John Hope Franklin

CHAPTER 3

PLOTTING THE JOURNEY

J OSEPH CAMPBELL WAS AN American mythologist who mastered the study of great stories. He identified a pattern we see in most famous myths called the Hero's Journey[4]. The Hero's Journey starts with a hero, the protagonist or main character of a plot in which the story revolves.

To sum the pattern up into the simplest of terms, Campbell says this hero starts in what is called the *ordinary world*. This could be considered the calm before the storm, where we get to know the hero and his or her setting before he or she hears the *call to adventure*.

This is the point in a hero's journey where the ordinary world is disrupted, and the hero must decide whether they are going to do something about it or not. Often, the hero refuses the initial call, choosing to avoid danger and trials that can cause pain and fear. But in a great story, she eventually embarks into the unknown, seeking adventure.

Adventure is full of danger and surprise; tests and challenges that introduce the hero to parts of the world she has not seen before. In a great story, a hero rarely ends an adventure unscathed, but also returns to the ordinary world with new strengths to use in later adventures. Campbell calls this the *Return with the Elixir*. This is what makes the journey worth it.

Almost every Disney or Pixar movie is about a hero taking this journey. Think about *The Lion King* and what Simba learned after losing his father, running away from home, and eventually defeating his evil uncle to retake his throne and rightful place in the world. Would Simba be as great of a leader without first battling hyenas? Would the peace of *Hakuna Matata* have entered his heart without first crossing a desert? The hero's journey is about leaving what is comfortable for experiences that build and strengthen a character.

So often, school does everything it can to maintain the ordinary world, keeping the heroes from entering unknown spaces and potential failure. Students sit in rows to control order. Teachers call it a classroom management technique, when really it is mundane-management, a strategy to prevent the unexpected. The answers are in the backs of textbooks to prevent any surprises. We teach the same content every single year because then we know what's coming.

There is a very wealthy school district in the county that I live that will not provide laptops or tablets to students because they are worried that new technology will distract from the learning that needs to take place. Not because of financial issues, but because the Internet causes more variables than a textbook.

A hero cannot embark on their journey if they are locked in a room without a key. And a hero cannot obtain the Elixir, their new strength, knowledge, character, wisdom or skill if they do not leave the ordinary world.

In an epic classroom, the teacher has to be intentional about outlining the hero's journey for students. I hesitate to call this "mapping" their journey, because there has to be- needs to be a degree of unknown in the classroom. However, a teacher can provide a structure or foundation for the journey to take place.

When starting to outline a project, you need to first consider what the ordinary world is for your students.

This is crucial for what the rest of your project will look like.

A teacher I know named Gerry teaches a cross-curricular Physics/Algebra II class. One year, Gerry had a class of very competitive students. All classes have their own flavor or brand to them, and this one could be characterized by their competitiveness. Gerry noticed that he had athletes, video gamers, and even artists who were motivated by trying to be the best at their crafts. Obviously, competition is just a part of what made up the reputation of this class to Gerry, but it was large piece of their ordinary world.

So, when November came that year, and the luster of the new school year was quickly wearing off and student engagement was going down, Gerry decided he wanted to utilize this class' competitiveness. He wanted to use what was already present in his classroom and the characters of the story, to create an adventure.

And so, came about the Great Pumpkin Drop project.

Gerry looked at a set of physics content standards dealing with terminal velocity and the speed in which objects fall when not faced with any friction. Using algebra formulas and properties found in physics, students would have to become masters at predicting how long it would take for an object to hit the ground from certain heights. For weeks, his students filled the hallways, standing on ladders and dropping things like golf balls and apples, timing the descent of the objects to the ground. They took their data and plugged it into formulas, and spent time discovering how the *experience* of terminal velocity related to theories and mathematics. All along, the students knew that the climax of this story would be one of the greatest competitions in world history: The Great Pumpkin Drop.

Gerry called the city utilities department, and asked if they would be willing to send a bucket truck to our school for a morning to help with a class project. He also called a local pumpkin patch to see if they could donate a couple hundred pumpkins leftover from Halloween.

And then, on a cold November morning, a 60-foot bucket truck pulled into the parking lot of our school. Busses full of area elementary students followed closely behind to watch the action. A news van parked next to a tarp where the rotting pumpkins would smash hard on to the ground. Four hundred high school students poured out the front door of our school to watch Gerry, the epic science teacher, smash pumpkins against the asphalt from sixty feet up.

But the physics/algebra II class was not laughing as their teacher dropped the pumpkins from the sky. They were not entertaining the little kids who shrieked and screamed as gourds exploded on tarps stretched across the pavement. They were not even lining up to get on the evening news and gain a little local fame.

They lined the tarp with stopwatches in their hands to see if their predictions were correct. Their challenge was to use math and science to guess how long it takes for a twenty-pound pumpkin to fall sixty feet. The closest wins and gets to revel as the master of terminal velocity.

A pumpkin-shaped trophy and eternal bragging rights.

And you would not have a chance whatsoever of having the most accurate prediction if you did not master the content. Therefore, math class had purpose for that month. There was finally clarity as to how algebra can be applied to something other than a quiz. Physics made sense in a way that it never had before for those students. If you ask any student who has taken Gerry's class what terminal velocity means, they will be able to tell you in a way that is not theoretical, but instead in a way that was lived and breathed. The equation, $V = \sqrt{(2 * W) / (Cd * r * A)}$, is not just a set of numbers and variables anymore. They are the key to predicting the rate at which pumpkins fall to the ground, and ultimately eternal glory.

I will be clear, the students knew that winning this competition was not life and death, or even a huge deal whether they won or lost. But they worked hard and with enthusiasm because it meant more than a worksheet that would end up in a garbage can after being graded. Because heroes like challenges- need them- and this is one they could embrace in the classroom. Their teacher devised a plot for them to succeed and fail; ultimately to grow in.

This project sounds fun, right?

It was designed to be. Gerry knew that having an epic outcome to this project, tying in a thrilling climax to the story and a competition to motivate his class, would create high levels of engagement. From an outside perspective, this project really might look like a bunch of time dedicated to high schoolers having fun. They laughed as they smashed eggs in the hallway. Half a class period was given to a trophy ceremony rather than pure content work. A whole morning was sacrificed so pumpkins could explode on school property.

But this project was not just created for kids to have fun. Gerry wanted them to be entertained and enjoy themselves, but he also wanted them to learn in a lasting and impactful way. So, what might come across as chaos was really a carefully planned and executed project; a story that was thought up long before a pumpkin exploded on the pavement.

Outlining the Plot

I once had an idea for a novel about a bunch of kids who were taken from their parents by an evil madman, who gave them a rare brain-controlling drug that was found deep beneath the ground in the Florida Everglades, and forced them to mine more of this brain-controlling drug, all to sell to the US government to give to soldiers, in turn making this mad-man very rich and powerful.

Bestseller, right?

I remember the day I had this "brilliant" plot idea, and rushed home as soon as I could to start writing the story. At first the writing was easy. My fingers danced across the keyboard, and the scene of the protagonist getting taken from his mother came to life. I went to bed that night elated, excited by the fact that I was actually writing my first novel.

The next day I returned to the story and wrote more, but not as much as the first day. Each following writing session, my word count dwindled and I wrote less and less, until finally, I gave up on the project. The problem was, once my protagonist got to his new prison and went into the Everglades mine shaft for the first time, I had no idea what to write next. I did not know who the other characters were. I knew nothing about my bad guy, or what made him so evil. I did not know how evil would finally be defeated, or how the kids would return home to their families. In fact, I had not considered how a whole novel could take place underground where there are no lights or oxygen.

My story needed to be planned before it could take place. Without an outline first, and some calculated brainstorming, I could not sit down and productively write my story. Unfortunately, I did not learn that lesson until later in life, and so this book never got written--- and the world is better for it.

J.K. Rowling spent five years creating the world of *Harry Potter* before she wrote a single word of the first book[5]. She invented characters and imagined details about them that made them who they are. Rowling devised the world of magic, and all of the rules of her imagined universe. She created a very basic outline of the plot of her story, and even knew how it would all end someday before she wrote a word of the first book

Of course, her outline was rough, and the story took many different shapes as it was written, but she had a map to follow along the way. Outlines are a guide to keep a story on track and help the author navigate through previously unknown territory.

It is the same with epic projects. Before every single unit, I create an outline that will guide my class through the story. Like the outline used by an author, it is rough and not nearly as precise as the actual story. No amount of planning can eliminate the unexpected, nor should you want it to. Plot diversions and unexpected twists are what give stories character and suspense, and tend to be some of the best parts of a story. However, planning the basic elements of a story prior to a project ensures that the plot can unfold and students are making their way towards something.

There are several key components to include in a project's story to make sure that there is a complete plot. The plot of a story and project serves the purpose of giving a framework for the hero to journey upon, and allows for key events to activate a student's mind and ensure that information is lasting (Remember neural coupling).

Every story can look different, and so every class and project should look different. So, before we start diving into the different parts of a plot and the important elements and stages of a project, know that this is not a formula that has to be followed exactly. The more you incorporate story into your classroom, the better feel you will get as to how those stories should flow and expand.

Creating an Outline

Your outline can be shaped like the plot of a story. In its most basic form, every story has a basic arc. From Aesop's Fables to Game of Thrones, stories start with an exposition (beginning), there is a rising action as the story develops, a climax or culminating event, and ultimately a resolution. Each of these plot elements are a heading for a project outline.

Your outline will contain details about what each of these elements will look like. As I have repeated and reused many of my projects over the years, my outlines have grown much more detailed. I often come up with new lesson ideas, professional audiences, and final products for my students, and so the outlines for my projects need to have a certain level of fluidity to them. But when creating an outline for an epic project for the first time, I make sure I have an idea what each section of the story will look like.

Here is an explanation of each element in a project's story arc. Once you have an understanding how each of the elements works within a project, you will be able to plan for them.

Exposition

The exposition is the beginning of the tale where we meet our hero and the world in which they live. It's where characters and setting are introduced, and ultimately where the journey (project) begins. In story, it is vital that the author or storyteller hooks their audience from the very beginning. Have you ever given up on a book after the first few pages because nothing in the story made you want to keep reading? Or have you ever picked up your phone and went back onto Facebook a couple minutes into watching a movie because you were already bored with it? The beginning of stories must be interesting if you want any hope of people listening, reading, or watching it to the end. The exposition of epic projects must be treated the same way.

I once met a teacher with an incredible project idea that had real purpose and an exciting authentic audience for his students to work with. Before the launch of this project, the teacher could not stop talking about the work his students would do, and how excited he was to see them dive into this project.

The teacher launched the project by having his students take a pre-assessment covering the standards for that unit, followed by reading an article about the conflict they would solve. That was it. That was how the story was introduced, and throughout the project, this teacher saw minimal engagement from his students. The students never engaged with the plot or really even entered it.

Upon reflecting with him, we determined the kids were not disengaged because of the project idea, or because of how the teacher taught throughout the unit. It was because the students never developed excitement and curiosity for the problem when it was introduced at the launch. If a student isn't invested in the problem at hand, why would they sacrifice their time and energy? If there is no connection to the problem, what will fuel them to make efforts to understand or interact throughout the length of the project? This teacher spent so much time devising an authentic audience and lessons to support this great project idea, but he dedicated very little energy to how he would introduce this experience to his students.

The beginning of the story should be seen as a hook or attention getter, an experience to draw participants in and make them see why the remainder of the story is worth their time. The exposition is the starting line, or the launching point for a major part of students' lives for the next days or months.

We have to think of projects this way, because when done well with purpose and authenticity, what a student works on in your class is a major part of their life. It is what occupies their minds at school. It is the discussions they have with parents around the dinner table. It can be late nights and early mornings as stress builds and deadlines approach. Your projects can be one of the only creative outlets a student has in their day.

So, the project needs to be treated as such, and you can do this in part by building up anticipation for the beginning of each project. I love to have an ongoing suspense in my class for upcoming projects. I had a student named Daniel who is a total film buff. He loves all things cinema, especially classic films like *Star Wars* and *Mad Max* – totally an old soul (No offense people born in the seventies, you're not that old). One day, as the World War II project was approaching, I walked up to Daniel and casually told him that he is going to **love** the next project. Then I walked away and said nothing more. Daniel asked why, and I just smiled and said, "You'll see."

Real nice, right?

For the next couple days, Daniel would not leave me alone about my short comment, and kept asking me why he will love the next project. I replied that he needs to just trust me, and that this project is going to rock his world.

He became almost angry in his frustration, and wanted to know why I couldn't just tell him what the project is. Other students began asking about the mystery, and I told them they'd just have to wait.

Suspense was building in the classroom.

Finally, the day to start the project came, and a Holocaust survivor named Diet spoke to the class about living in and escaping a concentration camp. This experience alone was riveting, and most of my students learned for the first time that people like Diet were even still alive, and more blown away that such people still live in our community. When she was finished with her story, I asked the class if they had any ideas of how we could make sure stories like Diet's could be preserved long after Diet and other World War II veterans were gone.

Most students' initial ideas were to preserve these veteran's stories by writing their biographies and taking their pictures. I loved their investment already and the ideas they had to serve veterans and Holocaust survivors. It was clear to me that having Diet launch the project had a positive impact and created an effective hook.

Then I looked in the back of the room and saw that Daniel's eyes had a fire burning in them. It turns out, the moment he heard Diet begin to tell her story, Daniel began to imagine telling it on film.

And that is exactly what Daniel got to do for the next month. It shaped the way he saw school forever.

Because aside from being a film buff, Daniel is also a foster kid, and being at a new school every few months for his entire life, and being distracted by intense anger towards his abusive parents, and having teachers tell him to pick his head up off his desk every time he *needed* to take a nap- has made him a less than exemplary student.

Daniel's experiences have led him to hate school. But projects like the World War II one has redefined this experience. Not only did he get to experiment with a new set of skills that he'd only viewed as a spectator before, but this story he got to be a part of seemed to be designed specifically for him.

And it was.

This is why the exposition, or the introduction of a story is so vital. It sets up an experience that has the potential to have a major impact on a student's life. Breeding suspense prior to the project was not difficult, it just took some confidence on my part that the project could live up to the expectations I was setting. You have to believe the effort of the project will be worth it if you want your students to believe it as well.

Not every project, and exposition for the project for that matter, has to be a bombastic experience that requires your blood, sweat, and your every waking minute to make it happen. However, every project should be treated with dedication and importance, because it is an integral part of kids like Daniel's story. And for there to be a buy-in, a sacrifice on a student's part to give their time and energy to something, there should be suspense leading up to it. The exposition is about introducing students to a new environment that they can embrace and be engaged in.

The exposition of a project should bring a noticeable change to the classroom. Part of that change might be the seating arrangement, based on the nature of the work the project brings. There also should be a change in the way you talk about class during the exposition of the project.

Make it very clear to students that a new project is beginning and the previous one is complete. It is very important that students know when a new story is about to start. It is almost like hitting reset, and allowing students to know that the previous conflict that they helped solve in the past project is no longer the problem needing to be solved. It is not that the story of the last project is no longer important, or that students do not still have skin in that game. Instead, as will be talked about later on in this book, projects should end with a resolution, an ending that leaves the participant satisfied. Your hero is ready to move on to another adventure (And you have to move on to the next unit in your curriculum).

Part of the reason for doing this is psychological. Knowing you finished a task to its completion is fulfilling, and most often gives you more strength, even though you have been working hard. Perhaps this is why school as it is traditionally known has this way of sapping the energy and excitement out of students. When one unit is completed, and tests and papers are turned in, it is simply time to start another unit with tests and papers to write. There is little to distinguish that a major task was completed. People need variety in their work, and it is no different with students and school.

The exposition in an epic classroom needs to make it very clear to students that a new, authentic task is beginning.

Verbally say this to students.

Pump excitement into the fact that a new project is beginning. I never tell students before the exposition what the project that they will be working on is. I want there to be a surprise factor to my class, and have there always be a degree of unknowing in the room. Your excitement during the exposition will be their excitement.

Project launches are also where conflict is introduced to the story, and students learn what type of work they will be doing throughout the unit. This starts with planning the **inciting incident**. This is also known in project based learning as the entry event, the event where inquiry begins and students start developing what the project will look like.

As described in the next chapter on Conflict, the inciting incident is the big launch that propels students into a story and gives them a real conflict and problem to struggle with and attempt to solve. Hearing Diet's story was the inciting incident for my World War II unit.

Rising Action

Following the inciting incident is the **rising action**, where we can finally get our hands dirty. At this point students know what the conflict of the story is, and they can now begin to brainstorm solutions. Students usually do the most intensive collaboration in the first part of rising action. Following the inciting incident or entry event, students do not know yet what exactly they will be working on or what specifically they will create. Therefore, individual students do not yet have a task list, and must rely on each other to create task lists.

At this point in the project, I give very intentional project work time for students to simply collaborate. Oftentimes this means them researching topics and sharing their findings with each other. When I order classroom supplies at the beginning of the year, I always stock up on huge rolls of paper. This is a great tool for students to create a visual collection of their ideas, and apply the use of concept maps in a realistic situation.

During the rising action of a story, students must feel safe to share ideas, and be willing to listen to each other. The teacher should be on their feet at all times while students are brainstorming, roaming around the learning space and interacting with the ideation that is happening. Part of the teacher's role here is to help come up with ideas or extension of ideas with students. However, more importantly, a teacher's presence is to help facilitate strong collaboration.

Remember, collaboration is not something that is innate to every person. It is most certainly not something imparted on most students from their time in traditional classrooms. Collaboration is a skill that must be taught and practiced. One of the key roles of a teacher in an epic classroom is to facilitate the development of this skill.

Be present. Ask questions. Help students build and grow in the rising action as they make their way to the climax. Once students settle on an idea, they can begin to vet their ideas using a process that we will cover later on. And then it is time to get to work.

When planning the project, try to anticipate what each day will look like. This plan can flex as the story takes shape and circumstances change. However, you should have a rough idea of how much time needs to be dedicated to content-focused work and how much should be given to project work. Sometimes it can be hard for students to delineate between content and pro- ject work time, and this is a good thing. The more seamless the relationship between the content and the project are, the better.

I have a project where students have the task of cre- ating their own lesson plans based on a certain set of World History content standards that I give them. For a month students are learning and mastering this content well enough to be able to teach the material to others. Their final products are polished lesson plans that they deliver at a local university to School of Education stu- dents- future teachers. The motivation behind this project is that my students are getting the opportunity to influence future teachers' thinking, and help these school of education students see that there are other ways to learn complex content than just lectures and textbooks.

However, before they can create engaging activities and go on a field trip to present in front of college students and professors, they have to do some research. And write an expository essay to assist in this research. And compile their research in a way that is understandable to everyone in their group. And they have to practice delivering this content to the rest of the class.

Students have to create high quality products to deliver to the professional audience. Partly because they set a goal in the story's exposition to serve these future teachers, but also because they do not want to go in front of a professional audience and look inadequate and unprepared. To create a professional, well-oiled lesson plans, students had to learn the content. A majority of project work time during the rising action of this project was the learning of the subject matter. The project and the content had a parallel relationship.

Other times there can be a clear division between project and content work time. During some projects where it's harder to tie the majority of my content into the project, I will have about an 80/20 ratio. This can change due to different circumstances, but often during a one-hour class, I will dedicate forty minutes to content work and twenty to the project. However, you must be very intentional to relate the two whenever possible.

For instance, if your students were doing a project where their objective was to collect cans of food for a food bank, and they were also writing an essay about poverty during the same unit, you would discuss the relation between the two on a daily basis. The task of collecting food will definitely not incorporate all of the same tasks of writing the paper. MLA format and correct punctuation have little to do with acts of service, but because there is some relation between the content and project, students will be invested in both. You just have to find ways to make that apparent to them. This will be covered in the next chapter.

Climax

The climax is the zenith of the story; the summit of the mountain you and your students spent blood, sweat, and tears to climb. When planning a project, and outlining the story, the climax is one of my first considerations. Rather than thinking about how I will teach the content, what the balance should be between content and project work time, or even how I will launch the project- I think about what the culminating moment of the story will be. From here I work backwards planning out individual lessons, designing the scope and sequence of the project, and how I will launch the exposition.

A chemistry teacher at my school had the brilliant idea of his students creating soap from raw materials and delivering it to a homeless shelter. He had some standards dealing with chemical properties of soap, used some prior knowledge of how his students could produce it, and then dreamed up what the kids could do with their creations. He did not yet know how they would get supplies to make the soap, or what lessons the class would need to learn all of the content.

But this teacher did know he wanted his kids to deliver soap to an organization that could use it. After having his climax in mind, he was able to do the necessary planning to make it happen. An exposition and rising action is much easier to write when you know your climax.

A story has to have a climax to make the work worth it. And the more epic qualities you can inject into it, the better. My class collected shoes for refugees. I promised them that if they collected a certain amount, I'd submerge myself in a frozen lake. Polar plunge. Hypothermia. History class. Epic.

A fifth-grade math teacher I know had her class create guitars out of cardboard and rubber bands. At the end of the project she lit candles, turned down the lights, and whole class had a jam session. Epic.

At the end of my poetry unit every year, we have a poetry slam at a local bookstore, where my students share their work with friends, family, and the public. It takes an hour and costs nothing. But it is epic.

A third-grade teacher I know has her students create arts and crafts in December. Right before the holiday break, they have a huge sale where community members (mostly parents) come and buy what the students made. The class then uses the proceeds to buy gifts for kids in need at their school. Epic.

One of the most integral parts of an epic classroom is having some sort of climax. Not because presentation is the most important part of a project; it's not. The journey is often way more important than the destination. Instead, the climax has so much value because it gives direction to the rest of the story. I would not put my two kids in a car and drive aimlessly out west for two weeks. There would always be this question: "Where are we going?" But if I said we are driving to the Grand Canyon, the hours of boredom, rest stops, campouts, and misadventures would all be worth it. Because they were a part of the journey to the final destination.

If you are going to have your students create public service announcements, actually find an avenue for them to serve the public. If they create videos, post them on YouTube and Tweet them out. Have students post their writing to blogs. If they use math to devise better public transportation routes in your city, send that data to the city commissioner. Create a climax for the rest of the story to work toward.

Resolution

The *denouement*: a French word for *conclusion* that makes you sound well educated when you say it to your students.

This is where you bring the story to a close. Every story must have some finality and resolution to it. The resolution is where the hero returns home changed and transformed, having defeated their demons or the demons of others. Steven Spielberg, when commenting on the state of Hollywood said, "People have forgotten how to tell a story. Stories don't have a middle or an end anymore. They usually have a beginning that never stops beginning." So often you see stories get so stuck on introducing more and more of a world and its characters that they fail to share how the world and characters are shaped throughout the story.

The epic classroom has to recognize when a story has ended, and give students an opportunity to reflect on their experience. There is an entire chapter on resolution and the reflection process, but be sure to budget time for a resolution in your story outline.

Turn, Turn, Turn

Screenwriting guru Blake Snyder, who wrote the Bible of how-to-write movie screenplays, *Save the Cat*, developed a rule for any story he ever writes: Turn, Turn, Turn[6]. He writes in his book, "It's not enough for a plot to go forward, it must go faster and with more complexity, to the climax." Essentially, no matter how much action occurs in a story, the plot cannot stay in one place, but must keep moving and changing in order to grip an audience's attention. Otherwise, the plot might have speed, but not acceleration. Think about action movies like *Transformers* or *Godzilla*. They may be visually appealing, and everyone likes to see huge explosions every now and then, but the same pace remains throughout the entire film. The stories do not have variety and suspense to keep one engaged to reach the climax.

This "Turn, Turn, Turn" principle must be applied to an epic classroom. I have done projects before where the formula for each day was almost identical. We would start with about ten minutes of direct instruction, followed by a short writing assignment, then discussion, and ending with project work-time. This project became too predictable, and no matter how much energy I brought to class each day, or even how compelling the project idea was, the work quickly grew stale. In a class where story is at the center, there has to be variety. When mapping out your project, ensure every day looks different than the last. This does not mean you have to think of thirty different types of activities for a thirty-day project. Instead, it means devising different ways of presenting these activities.

Plan a day where you begin class with a traditional lecture. The next day, find a video to give the information, and find appropriate times to pause it and interject. The next, maybe give a lecture, but illustrate on a whiteboard as you speak.

There are dozens of creative and engaging methods for class discussion. While it can be easiest to have students raise their hands and just share aloud with the class, incorporating other discussion methods can add tremendous value, and by experimenting with different ones, *and doing so often,* helps keep the class interesting and students engaged. Create an environment where students cannot predict what class will look like each day.

During project work-time, "Turn, Turn, Turn" can be applied by you coming up with different tasks for groups and setting deadlines for each of them. For instance, if a group is working on a video project, you could allot the first two days of the project to them brainstorming and writing down their concepts and ideas. The next week could be dedicated to writing their script and storyboarding. Editing, etc. could follow the next week.

My students did a video project in my class for a state competition where the month of time to work on the project was left wide open, and I did not set up initial opportunities for the plot to turn and students to experience variety. The unit was a free-for-all, and my hope was that they would independently figure out how to structure their time and ensure they created excellent products.

My students all lost the contest, and not a single one was even a finalist. My students learned that not everyone gets a trophy, and I learned that projects need structure, checkpoints, and some direction. Once students progress in an epic classroom, and they begin to feel comfortable working on projects and managing their time, the teacher can spend less time mapping out the specifics of project work-time. Students will learn how to create their own task lists and budget how much time must be spent on each aspect of the project. This comes with comfort and experience, and while more autonomous, students will still desire the plot of the project to change and the description of their work to have variety as the story progresses.

Epic learning is not a magic formula. While most stories do have some common structure, they are far from being an equation that you can just plug numbers in and make it work. Know that you *can* follow the outline of a project's story and insert all of the necessary elements, but the story is written in your classroom. Having an outline to serve as a guide is essential, but allow space for students and circumstance to direct your plot. The terms exposition, inciting incident, rising action, climax, and resolution can steer your project along and set the stage for captivated learning.

As a teacher, you are calling your students to adventure; inviting them out of their ordinary world into a place that is transformative. Where they can toil, collaborate, and create until they reach an unknown but alluring destination. Where they return with new abilities and mindsets that are confident and tenacious. You are allowing your students to become heroes.

"The harder the conflict, the more glorious the triumph."

-Thomas Paine

CHAPTER 4

CREATING CONFLICT

HAT IF THE NURSERY rhyme went a little something like this?

Jack and Jill went up a hill
to fetch a pail of water.
They filled it up and brought
it back to the farm.
The end.

Do you think you'd tell that one to your kids? Would it have the staying power of the original version?

Of course not. Something has to happen for that story to keep being told for hundreds of years. Something has to go wrong for that story to be a story. Otherwise readers and listeners will just exclaim, "So what?"

Jack has to bump his crown. Otherwise he'd never find out that Jill was willing to tumble after him.

Perhaps one of the most crucial elements of a story is the conflict. Conflict disrupts the ordinary. It gives characters a reason to act and break from the monotony of life. How can there be purpose without conflict? The purpose of something or someone can be found in the act of solving problems and conflicts that arise. Otherwise something just exists for the sake of existing.

This purposelessness has become a dominant presence in schools and classrooms. Students learn certain content because the government says so. They keep their heads off their desks because that is the rule. Students cram for tests because of the threat of a grade, and that information they studied so hard to remember the next day evaporates when the test is turned in. How many students work hard simply because their parents said so? And here is the scarier question: how many students *do not* work hard because their parents said so?

Is it any wonder why there is such a vitriol hate for standardized tests among teachers and students? Too much importance for these exams is to appease lawmakers, not students and educators. And this lack of purpose breeds disdain, low performance, and a lack of engagement.

For a certain portion of the population, school without purpose works. Some students are good at playing the game. The concept of self-promotion is appealing, and the challenge of achieving better and better grades is enough to make this minority of students work hard. However, this is a minority. As a teacher, I have encountered many students who are apathetic to grades. The reward for high test scores and A's and B's are not enough to warrant strong and consistent effort. And yet, this is the dominant tactic American education uses to motivate students. It is using a broken and ineffective tool, and the results are obvious.

Nearly twenty-percent of Americans will not graduate high school this year[7].

They are quitting.

And I think the main reason is because for more than twenty percent of Americans, this system that consumes over eight hours of a student's day, the source of so much stress and effort, the place that consumes the bulk of one's childhood- often does not have a relevant purpose.

Stephen Pressfield writes in his book, *The War of Art*[8]:

> *"In order for a book (or any project or enterprise) to hold our attention for the length of time it takes to unfold itself, it has to plug into some internal perplexity or passion that is of paramount importance to us."*

This importance can be found by introducing real and authentic conflict into our classrooms. Not the kind of conflict where fighting ensues or feelings get hurt. The conflict where the regular patterns of life are disrupted. The regular girl or boy becomes a hero. The student within a bubble, who thinks the world revolves around their habits, their music, their friends, their life- finds out not all is well in the world, and there is something they can do about it.

The work students are doing in the classroom needs real conflict. In order for the material we present in our classrooms to grasp a student's attention long enough for them to engage with it, it needs problems for them to solve. We live in a big world with big problems, and sometimes the issues students tackle are immense.

Chances are, there are people in your community who deal with hunger on a daily basis. Racism exists within your city or town. Homeless people probably live underneath an overpass near you. Believe it or not, slavery still exists, and these slaves are young women who are trafficked in every major city in the United States.

These are big problems that your students can tackle in math class, and in English, and science, and any other subject in school.

There are also conflicts of lesser global importance for your students to engage in, and those belong just as much in your epic classroom, because they are engaging students in learning so they can be prepared to tackle big stuff later on. Conflicts like debating about the meaning of justice, interpreting how something a poet said 200 years ago relates to the present, or creating a piece of art that lasts- conflicts do not have to leave the walls of the school to impact and engage students.

Conflict can be huge and conflict can be intimate. But regardless of its size and scope, it must be found in the stories in your classroom. When planning and devising your projects, one of your primary goals should be to identify a conflict for your students to wrestle with. Quite often, this conflict can be found in the content you already deliver. It just takes some new practices to uncover it.

I have a few World History content standards about a concept known as imperialism. They look like this:

Imperialism – Analyze the political, economic, and social causes and consequences of imperialism by: using historical and modern maps as well as other evidence to analyze and explain the causes and global consequences of nineteenth-century imperialism, including encounters between imperial powers (Europe, Japan) and local peoples in India, Africa, Central Asia, and East Asia (National Geography Standard 16, p. 216); describing the connection between imperialism and racism, including the social construction of race; comparing British policies in South Africa and India, French policies in Indochina, and Japanese policies in Asia (See 7.3.3) (National Geography Standard 13, p. 212); analyze the responses to imperialism by African and Asian people (See 6.6.3).

Exciting stuff, right?

When I start the process of planning my project and outlining the story, I know my goal is to think up a conflict for my students to work through. Once I have some ideas about what the conflict will be, I can begin to plan the rest of the project and conceive of ways students will solve it.

But before I can figure out what the conflict will be, I have to identify themes that live within these content standards. A theme is a central idea or point found in the story. In Steinbeck's *Grapes of Wrath*, a dominant theme is family bonds, or in *Star Wars* there is the theme of Good vs. Evil. The story of your projects need themes as well. They serve as a focus point for your students to expand from, as well as give an opportunity for them to grow in broad ways when learning specific content.

Without themes and underlying messages, stories are shallow and will not have a lasting impact. That is why you should try to identify a theme or themes within your standards before any other planning takes place. You must be able to answer the infamous question, "Why are we doing this?" before making students actually do the work.

For this particular set of standards, I see a theme of dominance of one group over another, a common theme seen throughout world history and many of the other content standards I cover in a year. I discovered the theme by closely reading the standards, using prior knowledge, and a bit of research in the beginning stages of this project.

Next, I needed to find a way for students to interact with this content. For them to truly engage with imperialism as well as the theme, I had to figure out what the conflict in their story would be.

I started with some more detailed research, and since this was for World History, the research was specifically about places and people listed in the standards. Here is a little bit of what I uncovered:

In 1856, the country of Germany began invading a very small kingdom in East Africa called Burundi. They started a century of pillaging the land, harsh violence, political upheaval, and outright stealing of Burundi's natural resources. They took over this land with overwhelming force, and forced enemy tribes who had very clear boundaries with each other to share space. This is imperialism.

When Europeans finally left this once rich and beautiful kingdom, it looked very much as it does today: locked in civil war and in a constant state of poverty. A direct result of imperialism. This happened all over Africa, and it is a contributing factor as to why many African nations are impoverished. And when nations like the United States send money, food, and unpurchased clothing from thrift stores- a small Band Aid is applied to a large gash.

The Age of Imperialism supposedly ended a long time ago, but the effects of it are still very present.

I did some reading, and now I've got information to work with. The next step is to write out all of the questions I have about the subject.

Why were places like Burundi specifically targeted for imperialism?

What does Burundi look like now?

How can we connect with people there?

Is there anyone from Burundi in my city?

What is being done about this problem?

Who can I reach out to?

You have to ask questions to find the conflict your students will uncover. You might not need to answer all of the questions you write down, but it is within this list that ideas can arise. After writing down many questions I had after my research (there were more than I listed above), I Googled *Burundi Grand Rapids* (my city), and learned that there is an organization in our area that works with a bank in Burundi, Africa.

Perfect.

So, I gave them a call.

Cold Calling

This organization had never heard from a public high school teacher before, so it was a little awkward at first because this was new territory for both of us. But I needed to find a conflict for this story, and finding one by making a few phone calls was well worth it. Sending out emails and making phone calls asking for help or information on projects is an essential part of creating an epic classroom (and epic community for that matter). Cold calling, or contacting people I do not know, is not something I was taught in the education program at my college. It can be very intimidating to reach out to people you do not know and asking for assistance.

Before teaching, I worked in business, and my primary task was business development. It was my job to track down business for the sales team and the rest of the company to work on. I had to pick up the phone and call CEO's and CFO's, asking for assistance from people who are in charge of thousands of employees and millions of dollars.

This task was daunting.

The first few calls I made were terrifying. I had this impression that I was being bothersome, and that I was inadequate for the job. My reaction to this fear was to find excuses to make fewer calls and contact less people. This obviously affected my performance, and my numbers were low as was the production of the company I was working for. My boss finally met with me to discuss this issue, and I shared the fear and resistance I was experiencing. I shared how my insecurities and feelings of inadequacy were getting in the way of me making the calls.

Instead of calling me a wuss or telling me to get over it if I wanted to keep my job, my boss gave me advice that sticks with me as a teacher to this day. He said, "Trevor, we have a good business. We are honest people with a useful service and we work hard. These companies you are calling on should be very happy that you are calling them and sharing our business with them. You are doing them a favor."

If you are an educator, you have a good business.

You have a classroom full of dynamic learners who have the ability to make very real and impacting change in their communities and society. Reaching out and asking someone in the community or professional world to work with your class is doing a favor for them. One, your students can fulfill a need or solve a problem that they have. And I'm not referring to a cute, "Oh that's nice. We'll post your students' artwork on the wall in our office." I mean that your students have the means of contributing in ways that are truly beneficial to the organization you are partnering with.

A social studies/science class at my school is working on an ongoing project to improve the water quality in our city. A girl in that class named Kenzie took the lead on marketing for the project and the organization our school partnered with. Before Kenzie started using her skills to market this project, the organization conducted a survey, and were only successful in getting around twenty members of the community to take it.

Then Kenzie took over.

Using social media, graphic design, and a lot of emailing, Kenzie was able to get nearly a thousand people to take this important survey. She attracted several news crews and city leaders to our school to see what her class was working on. Kenzie has skills and could offer services that no one at that clean-water organization had at the time.

The leader of this organization was so impressed by Kenzie's work that he offered her a paid internship.

Kenzie is a tenth grader.

That organization was very pleased a teacher at my school picked up the phone and called them.

Also, you are inviting people outside of schools to be a part of the fantastic and profound things your students are doing. They are getting to see the positive movements occurring in education, and not everyone is subscribing to the factory style of education anymore. They see there are teachers willing to break the mold and change what school is all about. So take hope and strength in that. The community wants to be a part of your classroom.

The community *needs* to be a part of your classroom.

You just have to pick up the phone or send an email to invite them.

Inciting Incident

In literature, an inciting incident is the event that begins or introduces the conflict. Every story has to have an inciting incident. If you notice in movies, it is almost always, without fail, around the ten to fifteen-minute mark. It is when Dorothy is swept up in a tornado, Neo learns about the Matrix, or when Buzz Lightyear lands on Woody's bed.

In an epic classroom, this is where the students learn about the problem that they have to solve. The inciting incident can take on a number of different forms. You could use a video to introduce your project, either one you made or one someone else made but relates well to the project you have in mind. It could also be a letter or email from a professional asking your students for assistance.

My personal favorite is bringing in a guest to launch the project. This is often the most informative, but also lets the students know that the project is real and the stakes are high. There is great emotional power in bringing someone from beyond the walls of the school into your classroom. Especially, if they are asking for help.

As a result of my cold call, a woman named Trace, who spent the past several years working in Burundi, came and spoke to my class about what she did there. This was the inciting incident for this story/project.

Trace worked for a bank called Turami that gives micro loans to citizens of Burundi. Normally, people in Burundi cannot take out a business loan because they do not have any credit to guarantee the lender would be repaid. However, Turami is different.

Groups of up to 30 people come together asking for a loan, say 15,000 dollars, and the money is divided equally among the group, each person receiving 500 dollars apiece. But the kicker is, they pay back the loan together rather than individually. If someone is short one month, the rest of the group pitches in and helps with the payment.

Communal lending.

This money is used to start small businesses: goat farming, brick making, clothing companies, or other small entrepreneurial ventures. And the beautiful thing about microfinance is that 90 percent of the loans are paid back in full. Meaning, that these businesses are working. People are making money. Citizens are being fed. Children are receiving education. This is not a Band-Aid for the poverty in Burundi; this could be what heals the wound caused by imperialism.

We found our conflict.

When my students heard Trace's story, they wanted to be a part of it. They learned about the poverty in Burundi- the problem- and heard about what one organization is doing to solve it. This started their thinking about what they could do to assist- the solution.

After Trace left that morning, I led a project-based learning inquiry activity called Knows and Need to Knows to start brainstorming potential resolutions to the conflict.

Knows and Need to Knows

The process works like this: First, have your students turn to each other and discuss what they learned from the inciting incident. You really want to give them ample time here to unpack the information they just received. These can be very organic discussions that grow from an immediate reaction to what the students just experienced. I usually spend this time roaming around the classroom and listening in on conversations.

Next, students share with the entire class what their group discussed. In front of the class, start a list of the things the students share aloud. This is the knowledge the students currently *know* about the project. The list creates a great visual that reinforces the ideas shared in the discussion. It also clearly lays out what the conflict to their story is. By doing the Knows piece of this process, students are hearing and reading what the problem is that they need to solve.

Encourage students to list everything they can think of during this process. It might take some coaxing on your part to create a complete list at the end of Knows. If the students are missing an obvious point to the list, ask questions like, "What are some things people are doing about the poverty in Burundi?" Or "How might the inciting incident plug into the content standards we are covering? Do you see any connections?"

Now students list aloud as a class all the things they *need to know* in order to make the project happen. Again, create a list, listing all of the needs the students think of. Part of this is listing all of the needs that they have regarding the conflict and information to create a solution. Who should we contact for professional help? How exactly does microfinance work? What can we do to help solve the conflict?

The other part of Need to Knows is the nuts and bolts of the project. When is the deadline? Do we have to have to write an essay? How will this tie in to the content standards? Do we *have* to read a book? (No you little whiner. You *get* to read a book).

You need to be very intentional in steering the Need to Knows process. Make sure vital questions are raised that can be answered throughout the project. Because once you have a strong list of Knows and Need to Knows, the project is ready to begin. By now, the students should have a strong grasp on what the conflict of their story is, and they can begin to explore different potential solutions. Burundi has been deeply wounded by imperialism, systems like microfinance have had some success, and they now have an opportunity to join in.

In your planning time after this class session, synthesize all of the Need to Knows into a few essential questions. These should be questions that are at the heart of the conflict, and if answered, will hold the solution to the problem. The essential questions are what will drive the project. I like to write or print out the essential questions and display them in the front of the room throughout the project. That way students can reference them and be reminded what the project they are working on is all about.

You can also use the Need to Knows list, and as an extension, the essential questions, to design your lessons throughout the project. If one of the questions is about how to use a specific technology, create a lesson about how to use that technology. If a question is related to the subject matter in some way, this is your opportunity to design a lesson that connects the project with the conflict. Only now, this content lesson has meaning and purpose. The knowledge students gain from whatever activity you plan is bringing them close to a resolution of the overall conflict. Additionally, these lessons and activities are tied directly to the Need to Knows list that the students generated. They are in control of the learning that is taking place; you the teacher are just facilitating it.

Back to the Project

The class established that the conflict in our story is that the Age of Imperialism severely wounded parts of Africa, specifically Burundi. After Knows and Need to Knows, we did some brainstorming to figure out how to solve this problem.

Here is what we came up with and then executed

My principal loaned me three hundred dollars. I was now a bank who gives out microfinance loans. The students got into groups of four, and I loaned each group 10 dollars. Their goal was to multiply that money into as much money as possible by the end of the unit. The students agreed that after they paid the loan back, we would take the profits and invest them in an actual group of villagers in Burundi who were applying for a micro loan. There is actually a really cool website called KIVA.ORG that facilitates this process.

After signing and notarizing loan agreements (by an actual notary public), the students formed companies and began holding bake sales, selling soda and lattes in the hallway, making bracelets, knitting scarves, and many other incredible small businesses to counteract imperialism.

One group took their 10 dollars and bought a bag of paintballs. This group then went door to door in their neighborhoods telling neighbors that they could shoot them with the paintball gun for every 5 dollars they donated.

They made 50 bucks. You can't make this stuff up!

At the end of the unit, the whole group (the class) paid back the loan in full, and we had a profit of over 700 dollars.

700 dollars made by 14-year-old freshmen. This is history class, are you with me?

My students were thinking outside themselves. They weren't sacrificing their break times in between classes, or their evenings and weekends so they could earn a grade. I actually did not grade this part of the project at all. They worked hard because they wanted to be a part of Burundi. They had a deeper understanding of imperialism than most textbooks can give, and they wanted to do something with this knowledge. This project gave them an opportunity to empathize and act; the conflict was real and gave purpose.

I had students write historical fiction narratives during this project. This is a skill directed by the Common Core standards. The twist I added to their papers is that their stories had to take place in an African country that was imperialized. Their stories had to be historically accurate, grammatically correct, and in MLA format- just like papers in a traditional school. The difference is, the papers they wrote for this unit related to this project they were invested in. When a student works on a task that is meaningful for thirty minutes, like the Burundi project, and then switches over to content work that uses some of the same language and ideas as the project, the excitement often transfers over as well.

Let's face it, some of the content we teach is not invigorating, just like many tasks in life that do not burst with excitement every time we partake in them. I do not care how many Geico commercials I see, I will never enjoy buying insurance.

Ever.

But we still buy car insurance because the process is part of getting to drive. If you want to (legally) drive, you have to shop insurance companies and spend hard earned money on a product you are not likely to use. The task is not enjoyable, but it allows you to do what you want to do: drive. The task has purpose and meaning behind it.

I find it very hard to make workshops or lessons on in-text citations engaging. The nature of properly citing one's work is just not that invigorating, and I do not like to teach it. And my students do not like to learn it.

But when conflict is tied into the work, and adding in-text citations brings you a step closer to a meaningful resolution, these tedious tasks begin to take on reason.

While students might not be able to fully articulate the task's direct connection to conflict, they can see that it does serve some purpose in them achieving their goals. Sometimes it will take work on your part to find creative ways to tie the task to the project.

For example, when my students wrote the narratives, I connected this content assignment to the microloan work with Burundi by explaining that working through the content, researching imperialism's impact on other African nations, and then taking the learning and synthesizing it into an original story; one is connecting more and more with the people who actually live in Burundi and are going through these experiences. We talked about how this learning brings about empathy, and empathy brings action. Action is what students want and are hungry for. Working hard on their paper is directly tied to this action.

However, I also made it very clear that the research that they do for their stories must be accurate, otherwise we are examining fiction and not really connecting with the stories of people in formally imperialized nations. So, to make sure we use only valid information, we are going to put all of our research through a critical vetting process, and give credit to the people who did enough credible research to pass our vetting process. And to give credit, we are going to use in text citations.

See what I did there?

Now, that explanation is absolutely true, and I really do believe citing other people's work correctly is a vital skill. But it is also in my content standards, and whether I could find a way to tie it to the project or not, I would still have to ensure my students knew how to cite texts by the end of the school year. However, I have taught this standard before in a traditional setting, and the lack of engagement that I saw from students was dramatically less than when presented in an epic learning format.

In a traditional classroom, the approach has been to drudge through the tedium because we have to, and if the reputation of a class or school in general gets marred in the process, we can always blame it on the subject matter.

"I know guys, in-text citations are the worst, but we have to do it."

Or does this dialogue sound familiar:

"Mr. _insert teacher name here_, when are we ever going to use the Pythagorean Theorem?"

"I don't know, but it's in the standards."

Not a very compelling argument, is it?

How many people have you heard from, possibly yourself included, who hated history class?

The most common reasons are, because it was "boring," or "the teacher just made us memorize dates."

History class traditionally has this supernatural ability to suck the fun out of the story of the human race. It does not make sense how the story of the world can be made boring, but textbooks and erroneous dates have succeeded.

Students in my history class are rarely bored. Not because I'm a magnificent teacher who has the secret formula to unlocking the wonder of world history, but because authentic conflict is integrated into every unit and project we cover. Challenges exercise the brain and stimulate the kind of learning that creates a lasting impact on students.

This is why meaningful conflicts need to be introduced into every subject area at every grade level. Even if all of your content standards do not align with the conflict in your project's story, any type of relation to the authentic piece of your project will help students to buy in.

That is part of the beauty of epic learning. The subject matter is still there, but it is absorbed rather than reflected. It's felt rather than just heard.

A second-grade class at Grayson Elementary in Michigan took a field trip to a local park that many of the students were familiar with. Only this trip was not about playing; this second-grade civics class had work to do. Much of the park was in disrepair and needed professionals to come in and fix things like broken elements in the playground and add better seating for visitors. The class took extensive notes on what needed to be fixed at *their* park, walking around with notepads in hand inspecting everything to determine what needed work.

They then returned to their school where they compared their notes with each other, and created an extensive report on everything wrong with the park. These second graders then learned how to use Power-Point, and created a proposal on how to fix this park that they all use.

Next, their teacher had her students write a letter to a local city councilman, inviting him to come visit their class and view their proposal to fix this park.

The guy visited them.

And a few weeks later, the students received an email from the councilman informing them that the city fixed everything that was included in their proposal!

That group of students learned at a very young age that their words have power and that they are capable of making an impact in their community. They also learned how to create presentations, and the importance of good grammar, and how to be thorough, and use creativity to achieve a goal, and so many other lessons that would only have come from real conflict in the classroom.

When students learn that a meaningful problem exists, their inner being is not settled until they attempt to solve this problem. We are wired to fight complacency and find better ways of operating in the world. School needs to facilitate this. Educators need to say farewell to the days of answering the question, "Why are we learning this?" with, "Because I said so," or "Because this is in my content standards."

Stories need conflict. Growth and vitality come from the challenging moments in life, when the normal world of a character is disrupted, and they determine that they must rectify it. Most of the time the conflict for your classroom's story is sitting right in front you, and it is your job to figure out how to present that conflict to the class.

At first glance, content standards can just look like facts and information. However, digging deeper can reveal a story within those standards and a call to students to leave the walls of the classroom. Once they hear that call, the project is theirs and they become characters on a purposeful journey.

But it's up to their teacher to allow there to be a journey in the first place. Honestly, this takes a degree of creativity. One has to be able to devise a story out of something that can look dry and bland at first glance.

Luckily, creativity is inherent in teachers. As previously mentioned, Sir Ken Robinson once said in his TED Talk that, "Teaching is a creative profession." Let's revisit that.

Teaching is a creative profession

Think about the amount of creativity that goes into your own personal classroom management, and the way you have learned to improvise in different situations in your classroom. How you've developed a look that can make bullies tremble, and another one that can send a child home prouder than they have ever been. Or think about the creativity it takes to talk an angry parent down, or to turn a classroom into a safe haven for your students.

Teaching takes immense creativity, and you can pour that same ingenious spirit and inspiration to introduce conflict into your projects. Make it part of your planning time. Give yourself time to sit down and do nothing but brainstorm. We have to get away from the mindset that school is just about delivering content and using our time to plan on how to deliver it. Content is important, and can still be a major target in our classrooms, but rarely is it enough to motivate a student to work hard and with passion. Passion and work ethic from most students must be derived from somewhere else. Otherwise you have to become comfortable with a bunch of students who are satisfied with getting C's and doing just enough to get by.

The other option is to inject authentic conflict into our classrooms. Make the time students spend with you every day be full of purpose. Foster an environment that makes kids wake up in the middle of the night with an idea to solve the problem your class has presented them with.

Conflict is good.

We *want* conflict.

Luke Skywalker lived a peaceful life on a remote planet, and his world was turned upside down by a man in a black cape and strange helmet. He had no choice but to set out on a journey to solve the problem that disrupted his life. No amount of self-doubt or Galactic Empire could stop him from embarking on this journey. It is in our bones and genetic makeup to solve problems and seek resolution. This is where great stories come from.

Like *Star Wars*.

And Burundi.

The Process

To sum it up:

1. Identify a theme in your content standards
2. Research the content to develop a conflict for the story
3. Find community partner
4. Write down YOUR questions. These are questions you anticipate to be asked during Knows and Need to Knows.
5. Create potential list of Knows and Need to Knows
6. Create essential questions

"Is this heaven?"
"No, it's Iowa."

Quote from *Field of Dreams*[9]

CHAPTER 5

CRAFTING AN EPIC SETTING

T HE FILM *FIELD OF Dreams* is about a little family in the late 1980's who live on a farm in the middle of the great plains of Iowa[10]. Their world revolves around corn; endless and monotonous rows of green and yellow stalks of corn.

Then something seemingly crazy happens: the father in the story (Kevin Costner) has visions and hears voices that lead him to build a baseball diamond in the middle of his corn field for the 1919 Chicago White Sox to play on.

The story is about this man looking like a crazy person for destroying part of his livelihood to build a baseball diamond for ghosts to use, and his journey to find meaning behind his actions. He finally achieves his dream and creates this mystical field, and in one of cinema's most classic moments, Shoeless Joe Jackson, the ghost of a famous baseball player, asks the man, "Hey! Is this heaven?"

The dad replies, "No, it's Iowa."

Anyone who has road tripped across the Great Plains might take issue with Shoeless Joe's confusion. He thought this *boring* and *monotonous-looking* state was heaven? Clearly he has never been forced to play the alphabet game for seven hours because there is nothing else to see in Iowa but rows of corn.

But anyone from Iowa knows there is more to that state than meets the eye. There is a subversive beauty hidden in those endless green fields. It is a place that on the surface looks like boring cornfields, but in between those rows is a stillness and scent made of magic.

This story has to be set in Iowa.

The plot requires it. If the story were to take place in Brooklyn, the events that unfolded would have been very different. The audience of the film might have still enjoyed the story, but the entire tone, feel, and purpose would not be the same. *Field of Dreams* has to be set in a place that at first glance is stale and lifeless, in order for the viewer to see that the setting is anything but that.

The setting of a story is foundational to how a plot unfolds. Its purpose is every bit as important as the characters, theme, plot, and conflict.

In a classroom, the setting is where the story of your class takes place, and is the backdrop for the characters to interact and the plot to unfold. It is what you and your class establish your classroom environment to be. If you want your class to be a story of adventure and excitement, but your setting does nothing to promote that, the story cannot take place. Teachers need to be very intentional in helping create a space where students can live out epic learning. This goes beyond how you set up the desks in your room or what artwork you put on your walls. The physical setting is extremely important, and we will get to that shortly. But before you can design how your classroom will look physically, you must first consider what the occupational setting of the room will be.

Occupational Setting

The occupational setting is the work environment an individual project creates in your classroom. It is the setting a specific project's story takes place in. For instance, when my students worked on the project where they created tools for refugees, my room was much more than a public-school classroom for that project. My students were immersed in a project with real consequences and the potential to create real effects in their community. The space in a typical history and English classroom would not be able to accommodate the needs the students had to accomplish their goals for this project.

They were using the back of the room to make phone calls to get in touch with professionals to help them with the project. A part of the room became an arts and crafts studio where students experimented with design ideas using construction paper, glue, and markers. There was a part of the room where students sat in circles and did something we call brain juicing. Juicing is where one student shares with a group a creative struggle they are having, and the rest of the group pitches in ideas to help them overcome their struggle. It is idea sharing, and it requires a quiet space away from the fray of the rest of the room.

This project also required a space for students to simply sit down and work alone. Every work setting, whether at school or the workforce should have this. Not everything is collaborative, and there needs to be space where students can be productive by themselves. Open work spaces are incredible and I am a huge advocate of them. Companies like Facebook and Google have brought this office environment to the mainstream, and have proven its effectiveness. But these workplaces also need retreats; places that are quiet and designed for the individual. Everyone has a degree of introversion about themselves, some more than others, and our classrooms must reflect that.

For this project, my classroom became a sort of social work agency.

This was the occupational setting for this specific story. The room did not just simulate a social work agency, it became one. Your classroom needs to take a different shape for the different tasks students are completing. When my students created World War II documentaries, much of my room became an editing lab. There were tables put together that students could create storyboards on using poster board. Groups put their desks together in a way that everyone could observe what their film editor was working on. A broom closet right outside of my classroom became a sound studio where students worked on narrations for their films. My classroom looked very different than it did when we worked on the refugee project. The occupational setting changes each time the story changes.

It is vital that students are aware of why the occupational setting changes and what new purposes the change creates. Much of these changes can be thought of prior to the project, but sometimes evolution happens when needs arise. A science class at our school assisted an organization to redesign the downtown waterfront here in our city. The class decided that blueprints were not sufficient enough for them to visualize the changes they needed to envision for the current waterfront. The students had ideas that they wanted to convey to the community that drawings could not communicate.

So they created a twenty-foot long scale model in the middle of the room. This thing was a beast, and was built out of a bunch of different scraps students brought from their homes. On the presentation day, professionals from all over the city came to our school to look at some of the students' ideas. They were blown away by this model as well as the proud students who stood by their portion of it to explain their visions for the downtown.

This was not part of the plotline the teacher for this class had in mind when designing this project. The project became a lot messier and required more time and space to make it happen. But he was willing to allow the story to adapt and evolve to meet the student's and the project's needs. This involved allowing the setting to change with it.

Part of identifying the occupational setting in your classroom comes from the realization that the work students do in an engaged classroom is more than just schoolwork. Whether students are working on a big authentic project like the waterfront design project, or trying to crack a complex math problem in small groups, what students do in your classroom must have meaning to them. Again, meaning and purpose are essential to epic learning, and the space must have purpose as well. This space has to be shaped around whatever students are doing, and must be shaped with them and their work in mind.

This is part of the reason I do not have a desk in my classroom. The work I do behind the scenes, like lesson planning, parent phones calls, etc.- is not part of the story students are creating in the classroom. It helps write the story, and even direct it at times, but I want my classroom- the entire classroom, to be a space for their story to unfold. Me sitting somewhere while students explore and create does not lend to the occupational setting. Me, the teacher, has to be willing to adapt if I want the setting to truly be for my students and their growth.

Epic Setting

The physical setting of your classroom must be devised in a way that allows students to accomplish the goals you have for your story and class. It needs to fit the occupational setting established by the project. Again, it has to have purpose. In a traditional classroom, one that does not always utilize the power of story to engage learners, the layout can be very industrial: rows of desk aligned in one direction. This fits the purpose of that classroom, which is to maintain focus on the teacher at the front of the room so that students can absorb information.

If the purpose of your classroom is to do something other than having your students sit still and focus, you need to consider what that looks like.

As the facilitator of this class, I have to consider as best I can beforehand what kind of spatial needs my students have for their story to take place. This process begins with creating a list. What kind of different tasks will the students complete throughout the project? Sometimes, this list can be long, as there can be a variety of objectives for students to meet. Other times, depending on your standards and the product your students are creating, your list might be short and not have as large of an assortment of spatial needs in the classroom.

Remember, this list is not concrete, and can be added to and subtracted from throughout the project as needed. However, it should give you a basic idea of the kind of work students will be doing during the specific project. Then it is a matter of using this list to design the occupational setting. Your room needs to be an evolving space. Perhaps one of the best uses of funding a school can make is to purchase mobile classroom furniture. Rolling chairs and tables certainly give students the ability to move around during the collaboration process, and mobile furniture also assists the teacher to change the look and functionality of the room for different tasks.

Many schools have not recognized the benefits of this kind of furniture yet, so it is up to the teacher to use what they have at their disposal to create the setting for the story. You can take stationary desks and tables and arrange them so that students are facing each other rather than the front of the room. Also, your entire room does not need to be occupied by furniture. Leave a space in a corner without any furniture where students sit on the floor and work on tasks that do not require sitting in chairs or desks.

I also have a spot in my room where we conduct workshops on specific content and skills. If through formative assessment or by student request I learn that one or many students are struggling with a certain piece of content, I use this space to deliver the workshops. Often, the entire class does not need the same amount of attention to each subject, so these workshops are usually optional for students to attend and are seen as resource for the classroom. Sometimes I lead the workshops, but often students lead them as well.

Also, the setting for a project's story does not need to be contained within your classroom. Hallways, commons spaces, and outdoor areas can be perfect places for students to work on projects. I have quite a few students who are naturally introverted, and the noise and movement of the classroom can be too overwhelming for them to be most successful during project work time.

Once trust is established in our class, and a group of students can assure me that they can work without my supervision, I allow them to leave the confines of my classroom. And to be honest, this is not always easy to do. When a project like the refugee one requires multiple stations that sometime pour outside of your classroom, there is the potential for a degree of chaos to be born.

Admittedly, it is much easier to have students sit in rows and observe me teach, but the kind of story I want to be told in my classroom cannot happen within that setting.

I once toured a school that recently underwent a 50-million-dollar renovation. The architect who designed the new school was well versed in innovative schooling practices, and turned every hallway into commons spaces. These spaces contain restaurant-style booths for groups to sit at and face each other. Each booth has an LCD monitor that students can connect their devices to and share what is on their personal screen. Inward facing couches surround tables for students to collaborate. At the end of hallways are long drafting tables for students to create large physical pieces of work on. They did away with bright fluorescent lighting and installed LED lights that promote an atmosphere of peace and comfort.

In the several hours that I spent touring this incredible school with commons spaces containing the potential for stunning stories to take place, I did not see a single student working at these spaces.

The hallways were empty.

The only time that I saw any of this furniture and space being used was in between class, and kids flocked to the couches and booths to have a break from the chairs they'd spent the past hour sitting in. So many teachers would salivate at the idea of having space like this to conduct class, and this school completely underutilized it.

And in the classrooms of this school are beautiful chairs that roll and rotate. If the teacher wants students to form groups, it is simply a matter of moving the rolling chairs and tables. To form a circle in the middle of the room for a discussion, students could rearrange the space in less than a minute. The flexibility to change the setting of these classrooms is remarkable and makes me quite envious.

Yet, on the day that I visited this school, in almost every classroom I walked past, these chairs and tables were lined up in rows facing the front of the classroom. The scene was no different than the rows of kids sitting in desks in schoolhouses at the turn of the twentieth century. Only in this one, the desks are shiner and have locked wheels on the legs.

This is a setting without a story.

I do not think the teachers at this school are consciously misusing this equipment. Instead, I think they were given an opportunity for innovation without first having the structure to support it. We see this all the time in education.

School can be very quick to change and slow to change. New fads arise all the time that offer the next big idea and solution to fix the education system. Some recent ones are 20%-time, Flipped Classrooms, Maker Spaces, and even Project-Based Learning.

These really are fantastic concepts and have the potential to make a major impact on students' learning experiences. But if there is not a foundation that supports these concepts and practices, they will not sustain. There needs to be policies and structure that allow for innovation to thrive.

For instance, take 20% Time, also known as Genius Hour. This is a simple concept pioneered by Google that allows students 20 percent of class time per week, one hour, to explore and work on a project of their choice. This is mostly unstructured time for kids to explore and create, allowing them to be unbound by the normal confines of school. This is a fantastic idea. Students are given a weekly outlet to express themselves and try new things. Entire TEDx conferences have been organized and executed because of 20% Time.

However, if 20% Time is the only period in a student's school week to have this freedom to create, explore, and fail- what is that saying about the rest of their time in school? Does this not diminish their experience in "normal" classes, and possibly even lead them to resent those teachers for not being like their 20%-time class? This methodology creates awareness in students of what school could (should) be, and therefore leads them to reserve their creativity for this class instead of all of the others.

I do think there is value in 20% Time and class with less structure than others, but I think it can be damaging to the rest of a student's school experience if this is their only creative outlet. I would argue that before a school institutes 20% Time, they should first evaluate their existing classes and ensure that students have opportunities for freedom and creation in those as well. There needs to be a foundation for innovation.

You can put the best beta-tested, state-of-the-art furniture in a school, but if it is used in the same way classroom furniture has always been used, there will be no positive outcomes from the investment. Kids might be excited to see colorful chairs that can swivel and roll, but the luster will wear off quickly if they are not used to create engagement.

There is no difference with epic learning. For a memorable, transformational story to be told in your lesson plans and projects, there must be a setting that allows the story to unfold. This does not mean you need state of the art furniture to give your students an opportunity for epic learning. Even stationary desks can be put in groups.

After the inciting incident of a project, I have a discussion with my class of what the room should look like throughout the unit. This starts with how the tables and chairs should be arranged. If students will be working in groups of four, perhaps the desks should be made into squares, with students facing each other. If they are working in pairs, should they sit side-by-side, or facing each other in groups of two?

Perhaps it would be beneficial to leave a spot in the corner of the room for them to sit on the floor in groups to collectively brainstorm. I've had groups of students who prefer to stand during class, and so I was able to get a high-top table put into our room with no chairs. Between the teacher's expertise and the students', you can create an individualized layout of your classroom for each story.

This is an opportunity to give students ownership of the setting of their story. Plus, after deciding what the room will look like, you can have the students set it up! You don't have to spend thirty minutes of your planning period arranging your room and creating the setting. The students can do it in five minutes, especially if they have a plan and purpose. Again, they are owning another crucial piece of the learning.

Vibrancy

No matter what content area you teach or what limitations you physically have to deal with in your classroom, the space needs to be welcoming to students. The setting of your classroom should be a place that students feel like they can let their guards down and be willing to explore and experience new things.

Part of this is how you decorate your room, and illuminate the walls, floor, and ceiling. Colors have a major impact on a student's psyche, and even have the power of dictating the moods they are in and how they feel. Psychologists have found that colors like blue and green bring calm and coolness to people. Red, yellow, and orange have the power to make someone feel warm and invited, but also angry and hostile. Studies have shown that showing a student red before a test consistently has negative results, as it raises frustration in them and alters their performance. Whereas showing a student blue before an exam has positive effects. Again, this is another reason we have to be intentional about the setting for our stories.

Changing the appearance of your room can have an immediate effect on the overall feel and connectedness of your students. It is more than just putting up a few motivational posters with inspiring phrases. It is being deliberate with the colors you put on your walls. I went on Amazon and bought a 10X13 foot wallpaper world map that I put on the main wall of my classroom. This baby is epic, and covers an entire wall of my room.

Since I teach history and geography in a couple of my classes, this has been a really great tool to have. I can use a laser pointer to point out certain places when having conversations with students, and they are learning geographic literacy by always having a map present.

But I have a laptop and projector in my room, and can pull up Google Maps in almost the same amount of time it takes me to pull out my laser pointer. So, I did not buy the map for that. I bought it because 71% of the earth is covered by water.

Vibrant, cool, calming blue water.

And the continents on my map are a soothing dark green. This map is a focal point in my classroom, and it helps dictate the mood in the room. I want each of my classes to be rooted in a calmness that can make everyone feel welcome. Even my very excitable kids (that's a lot of them), need a place that is peaceful and can be an escape from the noise and busyness of their worlds, and as silly as it sounds, I think this map helps do that.

If blue brings calm, and red can excitable/angry emotions, what emotions do you think white brings?

Probably not any.

Color is a powerful tool to give an intentional essence to your classroom, and when you leave your walls blank, you are not utilizing this essence. You can still have a great and productive classroom without putting color on your walls and ceiling, but you are missing out on harnessing something that helps create a wonderful setting for epic learning to happen.

Would your principal let you paint a wall? Can you put up removable wallpaper? Is there a thrift store nearby where you can buy a piece of old, colorful artwork?

The other walls of my room look like the refrigerator door of the parent of a preschooler. Whenever my students create something colorful in class, whether it was my class or someone else's, I have them hang it up. The monotony of my once blank walls makes a vibrant classroom that stimulates the minds of every student who enters it. It creates an animated space that again, the students own. And at the end of each school year, I take all of the student's work down so my next class can help create the setting.

Your classroom setting needs character and originality. I once worked with a teacher who *always* had a pot of hazelnut coffee brewing in her room. She rarely drank it, and the pot just sat on a shelf in the corner of her room. But every student, even ones walking through the hallway by her classroom, could smell the aroma of that coffee flowing under the crack of her door. The smell was always amazing, and it became as much a part of that class as the books that lined the wall, or the fact that the teacher did not use the bright florescent lights in the ceiling, but instead used floor lamps she brought from home with cool funky shades on them.

This room was inviting, and the students in those classes felt it. This was a setting where students could let their guards down and enjoy the learning that happened. Kids were excited to create stories in this classroom, in this setting, because it was designed for them.

Summary

What kind of stories do you want to be told in your classroom?

Once you can answer this question, you can begin to explore what the setting of these stories can be. Part of this is being deliberate. Choose colors and find art that make students feel like being in your room. Create spaces in your classroom that maximizes the output of your students.

Kids should not *just* sit in rows when they are in your room. They need to brainstorm, converse, sometimes argue, create, be alone, etc., and you have to give them a space that lets them do that. We also need to be aware of when we need to change the setting of our room to fit the story that is being told. Your room needs to have an occupational setting, an overall feel that fits the work students are doing.

All of this takes intentionality. Teachers need to think about what they want for their classes, and what they need to do to make it happen. But creating a setting in an epic classroom also requires spontaneity. Not everything can be planned and devised by us. We are experts at many things, and students are as well. Let them have some ownership in the setting in which their stories take place. Consider their voices in the layout of the room. Let them help decide how seating should be arranged. Hang their art, let them stand, make them coffee.

The setting is the place where stories unfold; where characters grow, and develop. It is not subservient to the plot or secondary to the evolution of a story, it is what gives the stories shape. Your classroom is a breeding ground for adventure, where heroes are born. If a team of World Series baseball-playing ghosts were to reappear in the early 1990's, it has to be on a cornfield in the middle of Iowa.

"Satisfaction lies in the effort, not in the attainment. Full effort is full victory."
                          – Mahatma Gandhi

CHAPTER 6

RISING
ACTION

I WAS ONCE ASKED TO coach an eighth-grade soccer team by an athletic director who could not find someone else to take the position. I figured, hey, I played some soccer in high school, how hard could it be? I went to Wal-Mart and bought a whistle, threw on a pair of Umbros that had been sitting in my drawer for a good 15 years (it turns out soccer players don't wear Umbros anymore), and headed out to the first practice.

I met my team, and then said, "Alright guys, let's do this." They looked at me with blank stares and one kid asked, "What do you want us to do coach?"

I stared blankly back at him, then chirped, "Oh right, you guys call me coach. Yeah… ummm… why don't you take some shots at goal for a little bit?"

"Who's our goalie coach?"

"Who do you want on defense, coach?"

"Should we stretch, coach?"

It turns out there's more to coaching than being motivational and blowing a whistle. And this was quite evident when my team got mercy-ruled in our first game. The mercy rule is when the other team lets you quit after the first half because you are getting beat so bad.

Of course, I felt awful and inadequate for the position. These kids wanted to win and dedicated their afternoons to this team, and I had no clue what I was doing. So, I started asking other coaches for help and advice, and watched many hours of soccer drills on YouTube. Our practices started having structure and discipline, and in our next game, we lost again.

But this time we were not mercy-ruled. And as the season progressed, the team started looking like a team, and I even started resembling a coach.

In the last game of the season, our team won and it was glorious. The guys ran around and hugged each other as parents took to their feet to cheer for their kids. The win had so much more meaning than if it would have happened in the first game. Of course, we all would have preferred the win then, but because of our toil, that final victory became a beautiful climax to a tough season.

The toil: the long practices, tough losses, and quiet bus rides home- are the meat of this story. It is the road that lead to the finish line; the reason why the climax of the story was great. The bulk of our soccer season, the good and bad, was the rising action of the story.

As a character makes their way towards the climax, working to resolve a conflict that has not yet been settled, there are different paths that must be taken along the way. While these paths may look different in every story, they are always at an upward incline, directing the traveler forward to the peak of the story.

This chapter is about the different paths students need to traverse in the epic classroom. Like the paths in a story, these different methods will look different in every project, and can be personalized to fit your classroom. Each of the methods are necessary stops for students to in order to have a successful ending to a project. Like all other parts of the epic classroom, you can shape these pieces to fit you and the story your class is telling. They're tried and true steps and processes that make the story flow, and help students create a successful final product and have a lasting learning experience.

Culture of Collaboration

The process of collaborating to achieve a shared goal can be a foreign concept and practice to most students, as they have not been asked to do it before. In many traditional classrooms, even asking students to discuss with each other rather than just to the teacher at the front of the room is a new idea. So releasing students to work and spend huge amounts of time with each other under the expectation that they solve a problem as a team can be daunting task. That is why it is vital at the outset of every school year, as well as every project, to set up a culture of teamwork and collaboration.

Group Contract

At the beginning of a project, before any work or brainstorming or project work can take place, students go through an accountability process. The first step is filling out a **group contract.** A group contract is a shared document that the group members write and sign. The purpose of the contract is for the group members to have a discussion about what they expect from each other throughout the process. These expectations are clearly written down by a scribe in the group. For instance:

I will complete any task assigned to me by the group.

If I am sick or absent for some reason, I will check-in with the group.

I will not use my headphones unless I am working on an individual task.

I will meet all deadlines that the group sets.

Then students come up with the consequences for not meeting those expectations with each other. This usually entails a warning system where each student is allotted a certain number of warnings or strikes before more serious action is taken. In my class, the serious action is a sit-down meeting with me, the teacher.

At this meeting, I allow both sides to share their grievances and defense, and I try to find a way to get the group back on track working together. Most of the time, this is successful, as most students need to just be made aware that their actions are affecting everyone else, and they will do everything they can to remedy that.

However, if the student who has failed to meet their group's expectations does not return to working the way they agreed to, they can be fired from the group. Being fired means that individual is removed from the group and must complete the entire project on their own. They cannot use any of the resources gathered from the group that they were in, but still have the same deadline and expectations that project deems from the rest of the class.

Sounds harsh, doesn't it?

This is not a punishment, but a natural consequence for negative actions, and it resembles the consequences of similar actions in the workforce. I make my students very aware of the firing process at the beginning of the school year when they first enter a project based, epic classroom. The reality is, students do not want to be fired from their group, and they do not want to have to complete an entire authentic project on their own. Thus, they learn how to collaborate and hold each other accountable.

This is why I can count on one hand how many times I have had to fire a student from their group. The group contract serves to prevent the need to fire group members, as the students access it and use it throughout the project. It is a reminder of commitments, and a way to bind one another to those commitments.

Project Management Log

The *Project Management Log* (PML) is a tool that coincides with the group contract. It is a task list that students reference every day at the outset of project work time. As a group, students discuss what needs to be worked on during that specific work session, and write down who is doing what. Therefore, everyone has a task to complete, and can use this log to hold each other accountable.

If someone is not working or goofing around with another group, a teammate can ask them, "Did you complete this specific task that you said you would?" If the answer is "no", then they can kindly ask them to get back to work. If the answer is "yes," then they can help them figure out other tasks to work on for the group. The project management log helps students learn to divide and conquer, and if used as a vital tool, ensures tasks are completed and deadlines are met.

Holding someone, often your friends and acquaintances, accountable can be an extremely difficult task. But it is a necessary one, as accountability is a skill a student will use the rest of their lives in their careers and relationships. If students are completing important work together in your classroom, they need to be taught how to ensure that work is completed with excellence. This begins with the teacher creating that culture, but also allowing the reality of group work to teach it as well. At the beginning of every school year during the exposition of the first project, groups write down in their group contracts the number of warnings that will be given out before firing. Without fail, most groups record that each student will receive around 10 warnings before a meeting with me, the teacher.

"You didn't work today; *you get a warning.*"

"You didn't check in when you were sick, *you get a warning.*"

"You've been on your phone all morning; *you get a warning.*"

You won't stop using your headphones when we are collaborating, *you get a warning.*"

Etc.

Etc.

Etc.

Etc.

Etc.

Etc.

Needless to say, by the next project, kids start writing down in their group contracts that they are not giving out any warnings, and that you can be fired for your first offense!

I of course then have to teach them about grace and second chances. But the point is, reality teaches them accountability, because if one person is dragging their feet in the group, it can have a dramatic effect on how much it slows the rest of the group down as well. Creating a culture of accountability is vital to the flow of the story in your classroom.

Brainstorming

The inciting incident is complete. The students heard from an amazing guest speaker, watched a compelling video, or read an intriguing article- and processed it in Knows and Need-to-Knows. The accountability process is complete and students know their teammates- and are finally ready to get some dirt underneath their fingernails. Most students begin to develop solutions to the conflict during the entry event, and naturally want to dive in and begin making their ideas a reality. However, oftentimes ideas need to be picked apart, dissected and ruminated by others until it is refined and is an exceptional version of the original.

Brainstorming is an important step of the rising action, and when done with intention and treated as a necessity rather than an obligation, can yield a student's best work.

Group Discussion

Individual group discussion should occur during every project. Students sit facing each other and share ideas they have for the project. Each group assigns a scribe to record all ideas that are shared- no matter how sensible or off-the-wall they are. The point is to get everything on the table and give the group a variety of options to work from. Sometimes the group can create a list of ideas, but another useful tool is for them to create a concept map. Once one idea is presented, they can create bubbles extending from that idea to build upon it.

As a teacher, I am *always* on my feet during this type of brainstorming, facilitating discussions and ensuring all voices are being heard. Sometimes if a group is struggling to come up with ideas, I will ask probing questions and even present basic ideas for them to build off of. However, it is vital that students own the idea their group lands on, and the role of the teacher/facilitator is to assist them to that point.

Brain Juicing

Creativity is like a stream flowing through a meadow, giving life to flowers, plants, and animals as it widens across the valley. But sometimes beavers stop it up with trees and rocks and all of those plants and animals die.

Okay, maybe that's a little morbid. But creativity does move and create, and sometimes seems to be obstructed, and no amount of will power can clear the obstruction on its own. And when those creativity bea-vers appear, which they always do for some groups during brainstorming, brain juicing can help students come up with ideas.

Brain juicing is large group brainstorming, where any groups who are struggling to come up with ideas sit in a circle and give each other assistance. The teacher often leads these sessions, at least at the beginning of the school year when this is a new concept, and students "juice" their brains for different concepts to help other students. This basically follows the belief that two heads are better than one. Since all of the students have a shared goal for the outcome of the project, they can lend ideas to each other and help them expand on them. Like group discussion brainstorming, I take my expertise as a teacher and lend ideas or expanding questions to stu-dents in need.

And to make brain juicing a little more epic, I usual-ly bring in a jug of juice to share, and float raspberries in the cups that look like brains. It makes a great conversa-tion starter when your principal walks into the room.

Workshops

Part of teaching in an epic classroom is about finding the balance between project and content work, as well as discovering ways to tie the two together. In my classroom, I call the time that is focused on content instruction, "workshops." The term workshop implies that that time is spent building and improving what we already possess, and helps prevent a dichotomy between content and project work. Remember, the more seamless the transition between the overarching conflict of the story and the nitty gritty of content learning, the better. The project serves to create authenticity in all facets of the classroom.

For instance, a geometry teacher could be conducting a project where her students are creating guitars out of cardboard and rubber bands. As students are designing their guitars, she can give workshops on concepts like faces, edges, and vertices. Each workshop can build on the last, and be applied to the final product, which is the cardboard guitar.

If the teacher knows that most of her students are unfamiliar with these terms and how they apply to the work that they are doing, she can give a mandatory workshop to the entire class where she is presenting new material. If, however, she learns through formative assessment that only select students are struggling, she can conduct workshops for just those students who need it. Rather than being lessons that are conducted every day to everyone at once regardless if they need them or not, workshops are useful resources that support the project as well as a student's experience in the classroom.

Sometimes workshops, or lessons, are for an entire class at once and are done under the assumption or knowledge that the information delivered is new or not understood for most students. And sometimes, workshops are intimate meetings with a few students where concepts are re-taught and reinforced. Regardless of how they are conducted, the purpose or workshops, or lessons if you are more comfortable with that terminology, are to grow student's knowledge and ensure that they have everything they need to continue progressing through the story and unit.

Tuning

When I was in high school, my best friend and I built an electromagnetic engine for the school science fair. Using the power of electromagnets that we assembled using old copper wire found in a garage, we invented a device that could cure the world's need of fossil fuels and save the planet from Global Warming. At least that is what we thought we did at the age of fifteen, and we had an incredible device to prove it. My science teacher liked our ingenuity so much that we were even allowed to bypass the school science fair and move on directly to the state competition.

This would be our huge break, and we dreamed of patenting our product after winning the gold medal, and heroically declining to sell our design to giant oil companies and make sure every person in America would be able to afford to drive a car with an electromagnetic engine in it.

The only problem was, we arrived at the state science fair having forgot to create a poster board to explain our design. And neither my best friend nor I rehearsed our pitch to the judges, and we rambled our way through the presentation and left out major points. And the battery we purchased to power the electromagnetic piston was almost dead when we plugged the machine in at our science fair booth. The stupid thing was completely dead by the time the judges came around.

Needless to say, my best friend and I did not win the state science fair, and we left that convention hall defeated; not by the other participants, but by our own lack of preparation. (We experienced a second round of defeat when Google was invented a few years later, and we learned the electromagnetic piston had already been invented).

Sometimes ingenuity is not enough, and success depends on more than an idea and even hard work. Every single project that has ever occurred within the walls of my classroom has been through a process to ensure the product's excellence. This process is called **tuning**, and it serves to enhance and augment a product or idea. Tuning can happen in large and small groups, and serves to provide students with critical feedback to improve their project. Essentially, a collaborative team of students presents the material that they are working on to an audience, and receives critical feedback from the audience to tune and enhance whatever it is they are working on. There are 3 stages to the tuning process:

#1: Presentation

The presenting group describes and displays their existing material to the audience (Entire class or small group).

During the presentation, the audience takes notes on what they **like** about the presenting group's material, and what they **wonder** could be done to improve it. The audience may not ask questions or give comments during the presentation, as this time is reserved only for the presentation group to focus on.

#2: Feedback

The presenting group turns away from the audience and cannot respond to the audience during this stage.

The audience first shares with each other (aloud so the presenting group can hear) what they **like** about the presentation's group project.

Example:
- I **like** how they use vibrant colors
- I **like** their use of images on the website.
- I **like** how their presentation is simple and easy to understand

Next, the audience shares what they wonder could be done to improve or enhance the project

Example:
- I **wonder** if they can make the font bigger on the pamphlet
- I **wonder** if their idea relates to the theme of this project

While the audience shares feedback, the presenting group writes down and creates a list of everything they hear. They will use this list to revise and tune their project.

#3: Respond and Clarify

The presenting group is given an opportunity to clarify and respond to any feedback they were given. Groups do not have to take advantage of this stage if they do not want to, as they can choose to respond with the final product that they create.

The Value of Tuning

The purpose of tuning is to use the collective ideas and feedback from a large group to ensure that each individual group does not miss important details on the way to creating a strong final product. When presenting groups must stand silently during the feedback stage, there is often a temptation to interject and provide clarity to the audience. However, providing a response is not necessary, as this process is entirely for the presenting group's benefit, and they can take or leave whichever feedback they choose. If the audience gives a piece of feedback that the presenting group does not want, they can choose to not use it.

Oftentimes, tuning reveals errors and confusion that goes unnoticed by creators. Anyone who has spent many hours creating something knows the propensity to miss details because of being so immersed in the project. This is why a second, or extra thirty set of eyes can be so useful.

Tuning can be used for different stages throughout a project. First, students can tune ideas and concepts that they developed during brainstorming. This can ensure that ideas are strong and relate to the theme before students begin working. I have skipped tuning product ideas before on projects, and deeply regretted it when students worked for two weeks on a product that was not strong or did not relate at all to the project idea. This was an error on my part, because I could have used the tuning process to prevent this time from being wasted.

Tuning can also be used at checkpoints throughout the project as products develop and need to be refined.

Whenever I am planning for my students to present their final products to a professional audience at the climax of the project, I have them go through the tuning process with their presentation. During this time, the audience is focused less on the product students are presenting, and more on the presentation and how effectively ideas are communicated.

Example:
- I like how they made eye contact.
- like how they smoothly transitioned between speakers
- I wonder if they can use note cards so they don't miss information
- I wonder if they can have better posture during the presentation.

Again, the purpose of tuning is so that students achieve excellence. It is one of the most important tools in a project, and can be the difference between a success-ful resolution to a conflict and students feeling that their work was incomplete. Giving critical feedback can be a very difficult task for anyone, especially students who are working with his or her peers.

It is the job of the teacher to model this process, and show how being critical can be different than being neg-ative. Join the audience during tuning. Praise positive work. Don't hold back what you wonder can be done to make existing work better.

I can't help but think that if someone would have wondered aloud why I did not have a poster board for my science project, or suggested I write down my presentation on note cards, I could be a rich and influen-tial inventor right now hanging out on a super-yacht with Leonardo DiCaprio talking about how Global Warming used to be a thing.

"Stories make us more alive, more human, more courageous, more loving."

-Madeleine L'Engle

CHAPTER 7

TURNING LECTURES INTO STORIES

T THE BEGINNING OF EVERY school year in my history class, before my students learn a single piece of content or even write a single word, we talk about why we are sitting in history class. What is the point of learning about events that have long since passed, and hear stories about people who died many years ago?

After some discussion, the class usually generates two profound, but common responses:

1. So history doesn't repeat itself.

2. So we can emulate, or imitate what was done right.

If we simply ignore history and all of the crisis', heroes, and villains of the past, we will lack the knowledge to make better decisions and be better people in the present and future. One could make a strong case for this giving birth to storytelling. Aside from its entertainment value, it is a tool used by people and civilizations to advance culture, simulating a progressive evolution. Joseph Campbell said that stories and myths exist to "harmonize," and "put the mind in accord with the body (for people) to form a way of life that nature dictates[11]." Stories shape the human existence into something better than it once was.

I doubt anyone reads *Night* by Elie Wiesel as a way to wind down and relax. We read accounts of the Holocaust to reflect on the violent potential of humanity, and live in a way that rejects that depravity. Hearing the stories of witnesses of the atomic bombs dropping in Nagasaki and Hiroshima are heartbreaking and even painful to hear decades after the event, but we read and hear them so we can then take every step humanly possible to prevent them from happening again.

Storytelling has immense cultural value.

A group of instructors in the United States Air Force realized this fact through their experience in the military. Military life is often steeped in storytelling and is the means in which tradition, culture, and strategy are passed down. Stories are shared on journeys to-and-from missions, during leave time, and throughout the many hours of sitting and waiting for action on military bases. These instructors realized how much story played a role in the life of a soldier, and devised a way to utilize it in training and preparation.

Methods were developed to deliver intense and complex content in the shape of stories. Rather than having soldiers just learn the theory of subjects like warfare or engineering, and how these subjects would apply in a real-life situation, the instructors created simulations with a story structure that the soldiers could interact with and be a part of. At the US Air Force Research Laboratory, researchers studied the patterns of stories, patterns their soldiers would be familiar with, and devised methods to convert the specific information that the soldiers needed to learn into patterns and scenarios.

Essentially the Air Force became more epic. [12]

Lectures

When the concept of innovating school is discussed and written about, there is often this idea presented that traditional methods of teaching are completely outdated, and therefore ineffective. The solution presented by many is that the concept for traditional education needs to be blown up and replaced with a system that is radically different. No more rows. No more textbooks. And no more direct instruction.

Much of the current education system is outdated, and many of the methods of traditional teaching should be replaced or adapted to a 21st century model. However, there are aspects of modern education that are still highly effective and should be utilized in classrooms. Sometimes in the frustration of rising numbers of high school dropouts or reading *Forbes* articles about Finland continuing to beat America at the sport of making great schools, we forget about those great teachers we once had who told lectures with flawless precision. Skilled orators who found a way to make boring content a little less mundane, and sometimes even interesting. You may be one of them.

The lecture does need to hop onto the conveyor belt that is delivering the industrial model of education into a garbage incinerator. Lecturing, or direct instruction, is an art form that has been utilized for thousands of years, from Socrates, to Jesus, to Stephen Hawking, to TED Talks. When done well and with precision, direct instruction is still one of the most effective ways for students to learn specific content. The trick is, how do you do it well?

We have all had the teacher who could drone for hours at the front of the room, forcing thirty adolescents to drool puddles on their desks as they slip into a boredom-induced coma. Charlie Brown's *WA WA WA* teacher was our teacher. We all laugh when Ben Stein calls out "Bueller, Bueller," because our names were called in the same tone of voice.

Chlorophyll. More like *Borophyll*.

Lectures need to be delivered in a way that the information sticks and knowledge is retained. And like the rest of epic learning, this comes down to engagement. For this engagement to be achieved with your students and for direct instruction to have a maximum impact, **you have to consider the format of your lecture, how students might interact with it, and how your lesson is delivered.**

Lectures into Stories

Neural Coupling is a phenomenon about synching up multiple brains. Even though speaking and listening are two very different activities, when a story is told, the speaker and listener share very similar brain activity (Recall the story about crying high school boys stuck on a boat). If the goal of a teacher is for students to comprehend and retain information that they the teacher already possess, then it makes most sense to deliver that knowledge in the format that contains the elements of a story.

Story-shaped lectures will look different throughout content areas, but all should share the elements of a story and have an overall theme within them. If you are a biology teacher and you have the task of teaching your students about plant growth and the biological mechanisms that are within this subject, you *could* present all of the information about mitosis and photosynthesis in a lecture that merely describes and explains these processes. Maybe by listing the process on PowerPoint slides, and methodically talking about each one. Or, you could craft that information into a story:

There was a farmer who lived on the edge of the Florida Everglades who grew orange trees. These trees were this farmer's life, and they were what kept the roof over his family's heads, put food in their stomachs, and gas in his truck. So, on that hot July morning when this farmer went out to his field to check on his trees, and saw that all of the leaves on the trees were withered, he became very concerned. His source of income was at risk.

At first glance, it looked like his trees were very thirsty. He checked his irrigation system, and found that it was working fine. He therefore knew that the trees were getting water, allowing for transpiration to occur, providing oxygen and nutrients to enter the stems and leaves and allows photosynthesis, and therefore mitosis to take place. Next the farmer inspected the bark of the tree closely, and noticed there was long streaks on the bark. He knew from past experience that this could be caused by a fungal infection of the tree. Fungal infections invade the xylem, or water-conducting tissues of plants and trees, and prevent them from receiving oxygen and nutrients.

After checking other symptoms of fungal infections, the farmer was sure this was causing his trees to wilt. Using soil solarization and the process of heating up the soil around his trees' roots, the farmer killed the fungus and saved the orange trees. His family thought he was crazy for coming home so happy after a normal day at work, but the farmer knew that his day was anything but normal.

This example of a story-lecture obviously lacks detail, but any skilled biology teacher could fill in the blanks and dive deeper into the content. When the content is wrapped into a narrative like this, processes like photosynthesis and a term like xylem is more practical and understandable. The beginning of the story about the farmer and his family captures the audience's attention.

A conflict is introduced early on that stimulates student's brains, and creates an automatic desire to hear what the resolution to the conflict will be. The delivery of content, and the scientific details are the rising action as the story approaches the climax, which is the soil solarization and the frying of tree fungus. And the farmer and his family lived happily ever after.

This is a story, and while not the most compelling plot ever devised, it has the elements within it to initiate neural coupling in young learners' minds. I possessed the biology content (thank you Google), and was able to plug it into the format of a simple story. This can take a little practice, but using this rough outline, information can be infused into a narrative.

Beginning (Exposition)

Introduce character(s), setting, ordinary world

Introduce conflict (What is disrupting the ordinary world?)

Rising Action

In-depth content that relates to the conflict

Climax

Problem is solved

Resolution

*Because of everything told in the story, **this** is the way it now is*

Also, be sure to plan to give detail and descriptions in every story you tell. Listeners' brains will process descriptive information in the same way your brain does when sharing it, causing more engagement and lasting learning. Paint a setting at the start of the story. A study found that effective lectures start with a 3-minute warm-up period, where learners' minds get acclimated to listening and learning. This is where you can lay the groundwork for the rest of the story.

Remember that every story must have a theme of some sort, answering the question of "Why?" Why am I learning this? Why is this important? Why should I listen to you instead of Snapchatting my friends? If you are telling a story/lecture about the order of operations, ensure that students learn why they are learning about this. Maybe have the character at the end of the story exclaim, "Now I can add, subtract, divide, and multiply all at the same time!"

Yes, I know this is a little corny, but students are in on the fact that there was a purpose to the story. Sometimes you can be more subversive with the theme, and let them derive what it is, but like some stories, you can sometimes spell it out for them. If they can now apply that theme to their own work, they too can add, subtract, divide, and multiply at the same time.

Not every story is packed with excitement or oozes suspense. So, do not torture yourself trying to craft a Pulitzer every time you write out a lesson. Stories can be subtle and simple; loud and extravagant. While differing in many ways, all stories should engage the listener, just as all lectures should engage the learner. So why not combine them?

Choose Your Own Adventure

In 1970, a man named Edward Packard was telling his daughters a bedtime story about a character he made up named Pete. Every night, Pete would encounter different adventures, and Packard would make up a new adventure for Pete on the spot. But one night Packard ran out of things for Pete to do. If you are a parent, you know exactly what this guy was going through.

So, with no ideas for what Pete was going to do next, Packard asked his daughters what the character's adventure would be that night. Each daughter came up with a different idea, and so Packard came up with a different ending for each adventure.

Choose Your Own Adventure books were born[13].

And it went on to become one of the bestselling children's books during the 1980's and '90's, selling over 250 million copies. The magic of *Choose Your Own Adventure* is that the reader gets to become a participant in the story. Rather than just absorbing the information, one gets to have a say in what information is presented to them.

Having your students interact with your story, your lecture, is vital. Direct instruction does not mean that the teacher is the only one who gets to talk. Teachers have to create opportunities for students to join the story and determine how it gets told. There are a number of ways to create pauses in your speaking and allow students to interact. Here are a few suggestions to allow students to be a part of the adventure.

Turn and Talk

At any given point in your story, pose a question to students. It could be what they think happens next, or a reflection of what they've heard so far. Then have students turn to the people around them and discuss the prompt.

Think-Pair- Share

Like Turn and Talk, you first pose a prompt to the students. However, before discussing with each other, give them time to think and process by themselves. Following an allotted amount of time, students discuss with each other, in pairs or group. Next, the students share with the rest of the class.

Sketch-Notes

Sketch-noting, or visual note taking, are visual stories a student creates when listening to a speaker or reading a text. Rather than traditional notetaking techniques, where it can be easy to regurgitate information in text and not actually comprehend the material, the learners sketch out what they are hearing and create images of the story. To be able to draw what one is hearing or reading, one has to have some comprehension of it. This encourages engagement with the story and active listening.

Sketch-notes can contain a combination of visual and text notes. The primary objective is for the students to create notes that work best for them.

Double-Entry Diary

Students create two columns on a sheet of paper. Title one column: "Quotes," and the other column, "Thoughts." As students are listening to the lecture, they write down any quotes they hear that stand out to them in the "Quotes" column. In the "Thoughts" column next to the quote they wrote down, they write their reaction.

Their reaction can sometimes be whatever is in their stream of consciousness, simply putting their thoughts on paper. They can also write down questions that they have, to be asked later or just to ponder over. The Double Entry Diary serves two purposes. First, it makes great notes for students recap what they heard and to study if there will be a test or paper later. However, more importantly it provides another opportunity for students to engage with the story. It simulates a conversation with themselves, giving them focus and making them think about everything they are hearing.

12-Word Summary

At any given point in the lecture, have students summarize important aspects of a particular section of the story in 12 words or less. While lacking detail, this is a useful way to make sure students are comprehending the key points of the story. How many words are in the average tweet? If a kid can pack a thought in a tweet, they should be able to do this.

Name the Story

Have students identify the different parts of the story. What is the setting, theme, and plot? What is the conflict? How do you think it will be resolved?

Be intentional with the story in your lectures or talks, allowing your students in on the fact that you designed the lecture that way. Knowing this, they will look for different elements as you tell it, creating engagement.

Energy

I know a chemistry teacher named Nate who treats talking about isotopes like the calling out of winning Powerball numbers. Kids do not hide their phones in their laps when Nate lectures about chemistry. They lean forward in their desks and connect with the excitement and passion that he emanates.

Students strive to understand what he is teaching, and race to demonstrate their understanding to him because they know he does this "shaking thing" when he gets excited and lets out a howl that you can hear from the hallway. And there is no better way to get Nate excited than showing him you understand something about science.

Nate has a way of making the content that he teaches compelling to his students. It's in his hand movements, how he darts to the whiteboard when he thinks of a way to illustrate a point, the different tones of voice he uses. He doesn't start his lectures with bravado, but works his way to the climax, speaking with a cool and calm voice until he reaches the crescendo. Not every student leaves Nate's class loving chemistry, but they all leave knowing that Nate does.

Personal passion is infectious.

Nate's secret sauce for delivering compelling, epic lectures is that he has a deep connection with the material. It's not that he has an expertise in everything he teaches, or that he is a world-renowned scientist and knows every detail about chemistry (although maybe someday). Instead, Nate is fascinated by chemistry, his subject area, and wants others to be fascinated by it as well. This comes across in how he teaches it, and many students adopt his same feelings.

Is the content that you teach in your classroom worth getting excited about? If you are nodding your head "no" right now, you need to begin searching for value in the material. Is there a purpose in the subject matter that you know will motivate students? Can you figure out a new angle to view the content that your learners might not have seen before?

The fact is, everything we teach in classrooms should have some level of inspiration behind it, otherwise we are wasting our student's time. Now, not everything we present in our classrooms makes us want to holler out loud and scare passersby in the hallway. I've said it once and I'll say it again, I hate teaching grammar. It is not an easy task getting students excited about the use of semi-colons.

However, I do recognize the value of proper grammar, and I take this purpose into lectures I present on the subject. Mike Rowe from the show *Dirty Jobs* once said, "Never follow your passion, but always bring it with you[14]."

I am not passionate about teaching grammar, but I am about stimulating passion for learning. So, I approach lectures about grammar with that same zeal and try to transfer it to my students.

You will not love or be excited about everything you teach in your classroom; nor should you be expected to. But you can inject zest and flavor into everything you present to your students.

Delivery

Storytelling is a craft that takes dedication and practice. How you deliver a story has just as much impact on the listener as the words you are saying. Your voice is a powerful and versatile tool that must be utilized. Monotonic speaking will lull people to sleep and force listeners to lose interest. Think of the teacher in *Ferris Bueller's Day Off,* or any number of teachers from your childhood. Change your inflection as you progress through a story/lecture. Start with a lower volume, and turn it up when the story asks for it. Animate the narrative to create an atmosphere of tension and then relief when the problem gets solved. Add sound effects that will make a student unable to take their eyes off you.

Feel free to feel a little ridiculous in front of your class. You will notice that students usually laugh with you, not at you, and they appreciate that you trust them enough to act goofy in front of them. Humor is the best way to destroy barriers between you and your students, and release a tension that can inhibit learning.

Every year I tell my history and English students a lightning-fast telling of the Industrial Revolution, summing the entire event up in less than 5 minutes, While I tell the story and relay the information, I simultaneously draw it out on a whiteboard, and have epic music playing in the background.

I rehearsed this story in front of my family several times the night before I told it to my students for the first time, practicing how I would deliver it to my students in the best way possible. The object of this story, my theme, is to make it clear that this was a major historical revolution that had significant impacts on society. I convey the theme in the contents of the story, but also by being loud and talking fast, and attempting the sound effect of the world's first steam engine. And by throwing my dry-erase marker at the climax of the tale; raising my hands towards the ceiling and asking the heavens if industrialism is actually good for the world!

I look quite ridiculous when I tell this story.

But at the end of the unit when I ask my students what they learned the most from in the past month, they almost all refer to that specific storytelling, and how it stuck with them.

I believe the Industrial Revolution is a compelling story, but I think what sticks with students from my lesson is the use of my voice. And how I pace the story, not giving away the climax until it is ready. And how I use facial expressions and gestures that help dictate what emotions my audience should feel. My students love hearing a story, especially one that is well-told.

Conclusion

A college professor named Percival Johnstone conducted a study that evaluated and measured human attentiveness, and analyzed how one's attention span relates to learning from long lectures. The study found that no matter how compelling a teacher is, or how dynamic and engaging the subject matter that is presented, the average student has an optimal attention span of ten to eighteen minutes[15]. After this span of time, there is a lapse where learners are not as focused and the information is not retained nearly as much.

In fact, another study tested students immediately following an hour-long lecture on facts that they learned from the presentation, anticipating that they would remember the most from the latter part of the lecture since that information would be the freshest. The contrary was true, and students retained the most information in the first 5 minutes of the presentation, and the worst learning occurred in the final segment of the lecture.

After 15 minutes, people zone out.

So, while there is still a place for direct instruction in the classroom and the art of a well-crafted lecture should not die, it might be time to kill the hour-long lecture. It's not that you're not a great speaker or your subject matter is not compelling, but humans physically cannot absorb information effectively for that long. It's futile.

If you read this chapter and are now thinking "This is great and all, but this guy has never taught an Advanced Placement class, and is ignorant to the fact that there is no way I can fit that much content into story-structured lectures"- you can take joy in the fact that you do not *need* to fit that much into *any* lecture. Because long lectures packed tight with complicated subject matter are ineffective any way you present the material. Especially in a world where students have powerful computers and game consoles in their pockets and purses, sitting and listening for 7 hours a day does not work.

Take the core material you need to present to students, craft it into a narrative, and tell them a story. Use the rest of your epic classroom to make sure they get the fine details. I got some of the best sleep of my life in a high school chemistry classroom. But I bet if my teacher taught me about radioactive elements with a story about superheroes or sea monsters, my naps would have been much shorter.

If we are always arriving and departing, it is also true that we are eternally anchored. One's destination is never a place but rather a new way of looking at things.

-Henry Miller

CHAPTER 8

THE DENOUEMENT

E DMUND DANTES WAS a bright, young sailor who rose through the ranks of the ship he worked on, and was about to be the captain of it at the age of nineteen. He was engaged to a beautiful woman and loved by everyone who knew him. For Edmund Dantes, life was good.

But then a group of Edmund's peers, who were jealous of him, framed him for a crime he did not commit, one that got him locked in a treacherous prison for fourteen years. During this time, he lost his fiancée, his career was ruined, and even his beloved father died. Edmund finally escaped the prison, found an enormous amount of treasure, and then spent most of his energy to seek revenge on all of the people responsible for his harsh imprisonment. It is during this journey of vengeance that Edmund started to do good for the people who helped him in his past, and at the end of the story, after feeling the depths of despair and pain, he is able to experience the height of ecstasy and peace. It is only through this struggle, through the hurt, loneliness, and darkness that Edmund Dantes could learn to live with peace and tranquility.

I might have just spoiled the plot of *The Count of Monte Cristo* for you, but that book is 171 years old, so if you have not read it yet that is your fault.

Joseph Campbell describes the ending of a Hero's Journey as the "Return with the Elixir." The hero undergoes a transformation at the end of their adventure, and can then return home with a treasure or understanding- the elixir- to share with the world. Luke returns home a Jedi who can defeat the Dark Side. Huckleberry Finn wins a slave his freedom. Nemo's dad learns to trust his son and take risks. The elixir can only be won through an adventure containing conflict and struggle. But this reward for endurance has the power to alter the world in which the character lives.

Edmund Dantes' elixir was an understanding that pain does not have the ability to erase love.

Each time you and your students embark on a new story and traverse through a plot to resolve a conflict, your characters are undergoing transformation. This transformation does not always manifest itself in a clear and obvious way, and can sometimes be subtle. But if students experience a story in your classroom, and you succeed in engaging them and activating their brains and neural coupling, they will have a transformation. A critical part of epic learning is helping students recognize that metamorphosis, and use the elixir they discovered on their journey.

If you follow the elements of a story, the transformation will happen by itself. The students, while having a variety of experiences and individual changes, will find some type of elixir. You will see the evidence of their discoveries in future projects and stories, but also in how they grow as people. Stressful projects transform students into people who can handle stress.

Projects requiring ingenuity and innovation make creative people. Projects with deadlines and a heavy workload help students become hard workers. The journey through the project should shape and mold students and equip them with tools they did not possess prior to the exposition of that story.

I rarely allow students in my class to pick the groups they work and collaborate in. I do this for a number of reasons, and regardless of my justifications, most of my students hate it. They naturally want to be with their friends, and often say things to me like, "My friends and I get along really great, so we would do really well working together in a group." While this is sometimes true (but often not!), working with someone you know and get along with is not always the most beneficial. When I choose groups according to different skill sets, learning styles, and needs, students are given the opportunity to stretch and feel uncomfortable. It is through this uncomfortable, often stressful method of collaboration that students learn how to hold each other accountable.

And how to deal with confrontation.

And how to divide a workload.

And many other valuable skills that can only be discovered through experiences that test and challenge. These skills are the elixir; a product of moving through a story. The teacher can create the framework for the elixir to be discovered, but the transformation of students happens naturally. However, unless this transformation is reinforced, and made clear to the learner, students (and people) can revert back to who they were before they found the elixir and unearthed new skills and understanding. This is why the reflection process at the conclusion of a story is so vital.

Reflection

At the end of every project, once a conflict has been brought to resolution and before another story begins, there must be a reflection process. Reflection can take on a number of shapes and forms, and all serve to sustain the growth that has just occurred.

Likes and Wonders

This serves as the tuning process for an entire project. First, students write down everything they liked about the project and why. What was engaging? What made you work hard? What content activities did you enjoy? The teacher can give leading questions like these to get students to reflect on the best parts of the project for them.

This serves two critical purposes. First, students are remembering and reflecting on what engaged them and learning more about themselves and what motivates them to work the most efficiently. Projects are not always fun, and as stated previously, they can induce stress and conflict. Therefore, the *Likes* writing portion reinforces the good that took place for students and helps them find as many positive moments from their work as possible.

The other purpose of having students recall what they liked about the project is feedback for the teacher to use on future projects. If many students write that they really enjoyed how you conducted book discussions, this should lend insight into how you lead discussions in the future.

When I taught my students how to employ a different, off-the-wall note-taking technique, I thought my lesson was a failure. I did not feel that I conducted the lesson well and communicated the concept of the technique to students clearly. But after reading and hearing from them about their *likes*, I received an overwhelming positive response to that lesson. Students raved about how they liked this new technique, and many shared how they used it in other classes. This was a cue for me to give them more opportunities to take notes in this way, and I planned those opportunities in future lessons.

The next step is for students to write down what they *wonder* could be done to improve the project in the future, for the teacher and themselves. This step is in my opinion one of the most important pieces of the entire reflection process. Similar to the *likes* process, students are reflecting on the project as a whole, and narrowing down to the pieces that caused them to struggle. This can get to the heart of what needs to be adapted and enhanced in the future on the teacher's part. It also can indicate for students where their limitations are, and help them conceive ideas to overcome those obstructions. It is vital that the students not only list their "wonders," but also write why they believe they struggled. This process can turn into an opportunity for students to just list their complaints and indict their teacher for any of their failures. But if you have them reflect on their "wonders," and try to find out why they struggled, they can begin to devise solutions.

Some sample "wonders" a teacher can expect to see are:

"I wonder if we can have more project work-time?"

"I wonder why the book we read didn't make sense?"

"I wonder if we could have more workshops on writing paragraphs?"

"I wonder if we could do more practice problems before the test?"

These questions can sometimes be answered in future projects, where you can give more project work-time, or allow more opportunities for practice. However, they are sometimes answered in discussions with students, where you can talk about the realities of time constraints, and now they can manage their time in class to work better. *Like and Wonders* should be formative, and serve the purpose of improving the project, the class, the students, and the teacher.

Story Lens

Following projects, I arrange all of the chairs in my classroom into one big circle, and the entire class sits down to dissect the story that just occurred. We use specific language to dissect the story, and I am very intentional about students realizing how the story took place throughout the project. This is our "story discussion," and my intent is for more students to see the project through the lens of story, and form deep connections.

The discussion starts with talking about the exposition. We revisit the entry event and how the story was launched. Students share about setting in the room at the outset of the project, and what the ordinary world was like before we embarked on the adventure. They talk about the call to adventure and how the conflict was introduced. The inciting incident may have been a month or more ago, and these details may need some prompting to be recalled.

We then move on to the rising action and climax, and students share their individual experiences of how they approached the climax of the story and what that final event or moment was like. This is not the same as the Likes and Wonders process; students are not giving feedback on the project and reflecting on what could have gone better. Instead they are retelling what happened, and what their group did on the adventure. Very often in this discussion, students laugh at the anecdotes that they share, and can get fired up upon remembering an old conflict.

They are practicing storytelling, and this ancient art can contain a full range of emotions. And at the end of our story discussion, the events of the project, the story, are embedded deeper into the learners' minds. By encouraging students to reflect on the project through a story lens, they are using language that activates neural coupling. The listeners are listening to the storytellers, and the emotion and descriptions that come with their tellings, and their brains are firing and molding in a permanent way because of it.

We follow this time of storytelling with a reflection on how they the heroes/characters developed. Students talk about who they were at the beginning of the project, and who they are now because of it. Truthfully, not every project has a life-altering status, and more than once students have snarked that they "are no different because of the project." But if a project does carry a certain amount of weight, and did possess the components to develop the characters in the story, this part of the discussion can be some of the best parts of the project.

Students get to share who they are continuing to become, and what parts of their environment has shaped them. This character piece of the discussion is a true denouement, a resolution to a story students knew they were a part of.

Celebrations

When the Cleveland Cavaliers won the 2016 NBA Championship, over a million fans poured onto the streets of Cleveland[16]. There were dance parties on every corner, rooftop, and even on top of port-o-potties. Police officers were giving high fives to people hanging off of fire trucks while singing "We Are the Champions." LeBron James and company rode parade floats through downtown Cleveland as two million people celebrated their victory.

This giant party was not just for the sake of having a giant party. The city of Cleveland had not won a championship for 52 years, and so when their beloved Cavaliers brought hope back to this rust-belt city that has limped through the past 50 years of economic downturns, there was cause to celebrate.

Hard work, patience, and diligence deserve celebration. When students accomplish their goals, and bring resolution to a conflict, they merit a moment to celebrate their achievements. Following every project, after the reflection process and any remaining content work (including assessments) I set aside time for my students to celebrate. Sometimes this is a donut party, or we play kickball, or play board games, or go on a hike. Anything that says to students, "Job well done. Let's celebrate your hard work."

I have had professionals visit and observe my classroom on the day we planned to celebrate the end of a project. If I was not able to preface to them what the class period would look like and why beforehand, afterwards they would ask questions like: "Why are you guys playing Twister during class?" Or, "I bet kids love this class. They just get to play. "

Yes, they do get to play, and it is a fun class. But there was a lot of blood, sweat, and tears that led up to this rousing game of Scrabble.

I have to explain to these guests that there is method behind the madness, and that celebrations serve a very important purpose in an epic classroom.

Reward and Motivation

Celebrations are the reward for hard work. From the very beginning of the school year, students are made aware that they will get to have a time to celebrate the end of every project- *if* they have reason to celebrate. The *if* is very important, because if there was a paper due during the project, and a student did not submit it in time for the celebration, he or she will have to miss out on the festivities and spend that time working on the paper. This is not necessarily a punishment, but a natural consequence for not completing the work. If one did not do the work, then one does not have cause to celebrate.

When students are approaching a deadline, a pressure and weight of that approach is causing them to stay up later, Skype with their teammates, and rip the hair from their heads. The celebration can serve as a carrot for them to chase. I always want my students to be intrinsically motivated above all else, striving to achieve because of internal awards from accomplishing a goal. But there is a reality that extrinsic motivation has power as well, and the lure of a class period, or even 20 minutes of celebration can sometimes be enough motivation for students to fight to meet a deadline.

Finality

Another reason for celebration I have to explain to bewildered guests of my classroom who can't believe I would take my students outside to play kickball during a rainstorm, is the sense of finality that it brings. As stated earlier, stories have to have finality. The characters must recognize when a story has reached its end and the project is complete. This finality, or closure, is recognition and acceptance of the conflict that students faced, and a transition away from the previous task to something fresh and new. When my students celebrate a project, they know their work on that task is complete, and that I, their teacher, recognize the work that they put in. If I do not believe we collectively finished the story and achieved our goals, I would not allow the class to celebrate.

Fin

I remember the moment I read the final word of the *Harry Potter* series.

It was pure anguish.

It was like saying goodbye to a new best friend at summer camp who I knew I would never see again. (Or at least that example worked before social media was invented). There is something bittersweet about reaching the end of a great story. For all the joy a tale can bring, every story must end. The climax must be reached and the conflict must be solved. Otherwise, it was not a story at all, but a collection of events and experiences. When you plan an epic project, you have to consider how it will conclude. Help students reflect on their growth. Revisit the journey, and talk about the good and bad that occurred. Write it down. Discuss it. Make sure the lessons that were learned are not lost like the information on a multiple-choice test, but instead are ingrained in students' minds in a permanent way.

And once you do all of that, celebrate, like a LeBron James fan on a port-o-potty.

"You are the hero of your own story"
-Joseph Campbell

CHAPTER 9

CHARACTER DEVELOPMENT

W HEN I WAS IN middle school, my sixth-grade class was called the Flamingos. As if starting middle school was not already a traumatic experience, we had to wear pink shirts on Fridays and our mascot was a goofy bird. I'd be willing to put money on it that a middle school boy did not come up with the class mascot.

The Flamingo teachers used an incentive system called the "Flamingo bucks," and would give students fake money whenever they did something good or meritorious. At the end of the marking period, there was a huge auction in the school cafeteria where students could spend their money to buy the latest and greatest products the world had to offer twelve-year-old kids in the mid-nineties: Tamagotchi pets, Boys II Men posters, Beanie Babies, and the crown jewel of auction items: a waterproof Walkman.

You know what I'm talking about, five pounds of yellow-and-black magic.

The teachers wielded a tremendous power, because the kids in my class desperately desired the title of having the most money at the auction, and therefore the ability to buy the best stuff. And you have to admit, the nineties had some pretty great stuff.

The teachers also had the power to take money away. If you failed to turn in your homework, or misbehaved in class or in the hallway, you would lose Flamingo Bucks and have less money to spend at the auction.

As a twelve-year-old desperate for attention and some type of notoriety in a big new place that could be scary and cruel, I did everything I could to earn Flamingo Bucks so I could proudly wear that Walkman in public. I stayed after class every day to stack chairs for ten bucks each time. I erased the board in Mrs. Bandy's class, turned in my homework every day in Mrs. Hueller's, made myself walk in the hallway when I felt every temptation to run. In this year of my life that was marked by my parent's divorce, having a voice that fluctuated its pitch every other sentence, and it being my first year in middle school- winning that Walkman became an obsession.

By the end of the marking period I had amassed 498 Flamingo Bucks, which according to my unscientific survey, was more than any of my friends. I knew without a doubt that on Friday, at the auction, the prize would be mine.

Then one day that final week, I was sitting in my honors math class taking notes as the teacher, who was a tall ex-military man with a crew cut as flat as a butcher block, lectured on and on about long division or multiplying fractions. In the middle of his lecture, I turned to the student sitting next to me and asked him a very specific question about the math content.

Okay, not really. I actually asked him who he thought was hotter: Britney Spears or Christina Aguilera. The point is, I spoke out of turn in math class. I remember as if it were yesterday, the math teacher stopped what he was saying, turned and looked at me, and said in a deep and commanding voice, "Trevor, I said there is to be absolutely no talking! You need to learn how to follow the rules. I am deducting *five hundred* Flamingo Bucks from you."

I felt every eye in the room staring at me, and tears welled in my eyes when I realized every single Flamingo Buck I'd earned that semester was gone. And even though I now know they did not, I believed every kid in that class knew I was broke.

And broken.

At the auction on Friday in the school cafeteria, they moved a table to the back of the room for kids who had no money to spend to sit at. Being two dollars in debt, me and three other kids from the entire sixth grade sat and watched the auction from afar.

Despite what I thought at the time would happen, the world kept spinning after this incident, and the embarrassment from sitting at the reject-table did not kill me. But this shaming seared itself into my brain more than any other experience from my time in middle school.

Being called out in class, having the reward of my hard work taken away without any chance at redemption, and then to be labeled in a very public way as a kid who cannot do enough good to even join the rest of class in an end-of-semester celebration, created a memory I still hold twenty years later. This story had a profound effect on the rest of my time in school.

Gone were the days that I tried to curry favor with my teachers. As a matter of fact, since the shaming, I hated this math teacher. I did everything in my power to get under his skin and make him pay for the way that he affected me. The experience taught me that hard work does not always pay off, and so why put in the effort? After a year of many detentions and calls home, I failed sixth grade math.

In seventh grade, I was moved down to a "regular" math class, as my previous year's performance proved I could no longer handle honors. Because I spent the last semester goofing off and loathing my teacher, I was unprepared for this class, and struggled again. This pattern continued through eighth grade, all of high school, and into college, where I failed my first two college algebra courses.

My struggles with math were always attributed to "not being good at it," or "having too much of a right brain." However, until middle school, I enjoyed numbers. I liked doing puzzles, and I felt pride in fifth grade when I went home and showed my mom I could perform long division. My war with math began in sixth grade when I asked my neighbor who his favorite pop star was.

The point of this story is not to paint this teacher as a monster who set out one morning to destroy my career in mathematics. Teachers have bad days, and make mistakes all the time.

I might be the king of teachers who makes mistakes.

The truth is, my old math teacher probably had no idea what impact his simple punishment would have on me. He saw a student talk out of turn and was not in the mood to hear explanations. After dealing with it, he taught the rest of class, taught his next class, then probably went home and played with his family, watched TV, and went to bed. He did not know he helped tip the first domino on my downward spiral in math.

Students are highly impressionable beings, and teachers are profoundly influential people. It is why members of this profession face such scrutiny. We hold a captive audience every single day, and how we interact with this audience can have an extraordinary impact on their lives and society.

I had an English teacher that same year of middle school, Mr. Peters. Mr. Peters asked me every day how I was doing, and often sat with me after class to talk about my parent's divorce. He told me about how his parents divorced when he was a kid, so he could definitely relate and be able to listen. He cut out time every single day to talk with and listen to me.

That is all I can really remember about Mr. Peters' class. But I know I loved every moment in his room, and in a very similar way he knocked down the first domino of part of my life's trajectory.

And now I am an English teacher.

There is no such thing as a story without conflict, just as there is no life without struggle. And in a great story, this conflict does not exist for the sake of existing. Conflict serves the purpose of shaping the characters of the story. Frodo was a different Hobbit when he returned to the Shire. Nick Caraway's black and white morals and ethics became much more ambiguous and jaded after living next door to *The Great Gatsby*.

Characters are not stagnant figures who traverse through a plot; instead they develop and shape according to the events occurring in the setting they journey through.

The same applies to our students when we view them as characters in an ongoing story. They are fluid beings influenced and crafted by their surroundings, and how a teacher approaches their classroom environment plays a fundamental role in how these characters develop. Whether intentional or not, how I was treated and engaged in those two middle school classrooms had a profound effect on who I grew up to be. Again, the effect we have on students, and people in general is not always calculated.

There is no such thing as a perfect educator, and our imperfections do play a role in the characters in the stories unfolding in our classrooms. However, you can approach the stories in the classroom with the knowledge that your students are characters, and the conflict that arises in school should shape them in a positive way.

Once during a reflection exercise at the end of my Industrialism Unit, where students spent hours upon hours creating tools for refugees, I asked my students what they liked about the project and if there was anything that could be done better next time the project takes place. A girl raised her hand and matter-of-factly asked, "I wonder why we just spent a month doing the work someone (social workers) gets paid to do?"

Essentially, why are we working for free?

I was stunned. The feedback from the other students was this immense gratification that they could help people who needed the assistance. And yet this student could not comprehend why she worked hard for someone else without any financial gain.

At first I was incredulous and honestly a little disgusted by this girl's attitude following a great service project. She saw people come from the depths of the world's poverty and struggle to exist in a new and modern land, and yet all she could consider was that she did not get paid.

But then I forced myself to pause and reflect, and realized this girl had never served anyone before. No one ever taught her to or gave her the opportunity to get her hands dirty and feel stress for someone else. Helping a group of strangers was a foreign concept to her, and so a natural inclination towards selfishness was her reaction.

My response to her question was, "Because that's what we do in this class. We serve others." I received a major eye roll for that, and even had to answer the girl's question again when it came from her parents at conferences later in the fall.

But I did keep having my class do service projects throughout the year. They held shoe drives and wrote children's books for kids in Haiti. They created stories for veterans and picked up trash around the campus of our school. We continually poured our strength and energy into helping others.

At the end of the school year, I have my students write a letter to next year's freshmen, giving them any advice as they start their high school journey. That same girl wrote in her letter: "At first you might not like doing all these projects for other people. But trust me, it's worth it."

This character developed.

She started her journey in my classroom resistant to change, struggling with the ability to empathize and see the world outside of herself. This trait limited her, and kept her confined in a bubble that would not let her experience some of the wonders of the journey that she is on. Part of her condition then was her fault, but mostly as a cause from the setting she grew up in. She was taught to be narrow, and was prevented from growing and experiencing the joy of serving others.

This girl needed conflict to break into a new form. She began the Hero's Journey resistant to change, but eventually underwent a transformation that is irreversible. The projects throughout the year, and the constant exposure to problems that needed to be solved, and an environment that encourages service grew and stretched her.

There is always a temptation with difficult students to lose patience in them. I admittedly left class the day the girl snarked about not getting paid to help people, and told other teachers about it as if she was a lost cause. So often when teachers see this kind of behavior from students, disinterest and resistance, they shift their focus to other students who are interested and do not resist the experiences you are bringing them.

However, if we truly believe that students are characters in an unfolding plot, we have to believe they will develop like all characters do. This requires patience and diligence on the teacher's part, and the willingness to see students as characters who are evolving; undergoing a lasting transformation. The question becomes, how can teachers ensure the characters in the story, their students, are evolving in a positive way?

Leaving the Comfort Zone

Back when *The Hunger Games* was the #1 New York Times bestseller and Jennifer Lawrence had signed up to play the protagonist and bring the most popular book in the world to life, I was a new teacher who wanted to grasp my students' attention. Instead of reading a book like *Animal Farm* or *1984* during the Cold War Unit, I decided that the class would read *The Hunger Games* and learn about police states through a narrative about teenagers hunting each other. I figured this choice of reading would engage everyone in the room, and in turn have them invest in everything else going on throughout the unit.

I also wanted to be the cool teacher (Remember your first year of teaching?)

Unfortunately, my plan backfired. Nearly every student in my classroom had already read the book, and the ones who had not were intrigued by the plot, but reminded of the many other young adult post-apocalyptic novels that had come out in that same span of time. For *most* of the students, the reading was not challenging, and I largely failed at connecting the reading with the content I wanted my students to derive from it.

I chose the book because I believed it would create easy-to-access engagement. I have learned since that it is rare to find deep and connective learning on the easy route. Growth happens when students are stretched beyond their comfort zones, brought out of the ordinary world into unknown territory. This is evident in so many aspects of life. Think of the most transformative periods of your own life. Were they all joyous events that you celebrated immediately after? Or were they more like forest fires- destructive, painful, and challenging experiences that created very real damage in order to allow new and stronger growth?

Very little growth happens in the alpine, at the peak of mountains when you stand on top of the world. The scenery might be beautiful from that vantage point, but there are not trees growing at the summit. Growth happens in the valley, where the hard work is taking place. Serving refugees and trudging her way towards a deadline was the valley for that one girl in my class. Collaborating with a group of students who are not your friends is what stretches many of my students and forces them to learn teamwork. Reading fiction that was written for a different generation and finding relevant meaning in it can be strenuous work. But it is this stretching, this escape from the comfortable bubbles that school often fosters, where real character development begins.

Encouragement

One of the most impactful ways to encourage character development in your students is to reinforce positive and productive behavior. Words of encouragement can be the most powerful and effective tools in a teacher's tool belt, and when used with purpose, can have a dramatic effect on students.

I had a student named Steven who was apathetic to almost every aspect of my class. He tried to sleep when I was not looking, turned in very little work, and never spoke up in class discussion. Steven exhibited behavior teachers see all the time in classrooms, and this behavior wears on one's patience. It definitely wore on mine.

After months of pouring into Steven and attempting to coax him into working using incentives, making him aware of the consequences of poor grades, and calling his mother and letting her know how little progress I was seeing – I still saw minimal growth from him. Steven was getting too close to having a failing grade that could not be recovered.

And then one day we were having a class discussion about the effects of violent video games on society, and Steven's head sprang up from his desk and his hand rose into the air. Steven spouted off a two-minute monologue about how video games are not the problem, providing research to prove it, delivering his impromptu speech with a burning passion.

I was floored. This kid said more words in that two-minute span than I had literally heard him say the entire school year. I called his mom later that day and told her about him speaking up in class and how proud I was of him, and she thanked me and hung up. The next day, Steven came right up to me and thanked me for calling his mom, and told me she was "so happy with him the entire evening and even this morning!"

Later that day, Steven spoke up again in class discussion, and this time it was not even about video games. A trend had begun, and Steven started sleeping less in class and working more. He walked taller, talked more, and started believing in himself.

Then he passed my class.

Teachers wield a capacity for destruction, but even more so, for so much good. Calling Steven's mother took thirty seconds of my time, and yet the impact of my phone call had an eternal effect on Steven's life. Speaking up in class discussion can seem like an easy and menial task for someone who is experienced in it, but for Steven it took courage. Courage should be praised. Steven did not suddenly become an A student after this event, nor is he one now. But he is not an F-student either, and he was one for a long time. The truth is, he needed time to develop, and that was not going to happen if teachers did not show him grace, have patience, and encourage his growth.

Students need to know when they are acting and performing in a way that is moving them forward and not backward. Sometimes this is by me making a phone call home, but mostly through short one-on-one interactions. At a graduation ceremony, a senior approached me and told me one of the greatest moments in his high school career was when I told him during his freshmen year that I was proud of a poem he wrote.

I have NO recollection of his poem or praising him.

But he did. And because he was a member of my captive audience, and that I had already earned his respect, that praise carried weight. This is not to say that positive encouragement should be dealt out in abundance without real cause. Not every good deed deserves a trophy, and too many trophies subtract from the significance of one that was well-earned. However, a statement that uplifts a student and recognizes real growth can have an immense effect on them. Part of developing strong characters in your classroom is to realize that.

Failure

The summer after my senior year of high school, I got in some trouble.

Like a lot of trouble.

The kind of trouble where the police have to take your mugshot for possessing a certain kind of cigarette, and you have to find a new set of friends who make better choices.

A decade later, a group of students in my class Googled my name (which is kind of weird), and they found that said mugshot. In the middle of a grammar lesson, one of those kids cracked a malicious grin, then raised his hand and said, "Mr. Muir, did you get arrested?"

My heart stopped. My principal was aware of the mistake I made as a teenager, but up to this point, my students had no idea that I was a mistake-making human being. To them, I lived under a desk in my classroom and ate dinner every night in the school cafeteria. If I happened to run into any of them at the grocery store, they assumed I was shopping for a class project.

But now they saw that I bled, and every instinct of mine told me to blow it off and tell them it wasn't me in the picture. Or maybe force a temper and tell that kid to mind his own business, and reinforce to the class that my private affairs do not concern them. I also considered lying and creating an elaborate story of how I was arrested for silently protesting or something else that was noble and good.

Instead I decided to tell the truth.

I let my students into a difficult period of my adolescence, and told them how choices that I made as a teenager had major consequences on me then, and that those consequences follow me to this day. I did not make excuses for my choices, but instead shed light on why I made them, and how I ultimately experienced real, tangible; painful failure.

I also talked about redemption, and how I learned more about myself from that failure than I ever did from my successes. Grammar was put on the backburner for the rest of that class period, and the students shared story after story with each other and me about times they failed and how they have grown from that. At the end of that class period, we decided as a class that we would embrace our failures. Instead of existing in an environment where failure was rejected and the cause of shame, we would create a place where failing was seen as an experience to be reflected on and learned from.

Failure should not be hiding in closets or left at home where no one can see it. It is such a temptation of teachers to hide their lives from students and gloss over the low moments of our own lives. In doing so, we create an environment in which our students do the same, and have a fear of failing; thereby giving themselves less opportunities to succeed.

Ralph Heath, the author of *Celebrating Failure: The Power of Taking Risks, Making Mistakes and Thinking Big*, wrote[17]:

> "Failure and defeat are life's greatest teachers [but] sadly, most people don't want to go there. Instead they choose to play it safe, to fly below the radar, repeating the same safe choices over and over again. They operate under the belief that if they make no waves, they attract no attention; no one will yell at them for failing because they generally never attempt anything great at which they could possibly fail (or succeed)."

How can the protagonists of the stories unfolding in your classroom, the heroes whose job it is to solve the conflict and return new and evolved people, do any of these things if not given opportunities to fail? This culture of failure must be fostered to exist. Traditional schooling, with letter grades, badge systems, and other incentive programs, have served to create a place that is abject to failure, so one must be intentional to allow it and teach students to learn from it.

We did a project where students used content standards to create board games that would be played by kids at a local elementary school. Judging by the unique ideas and artistic creations, I thought my students had excellent pieces of work to present to their target audience-young children. However, when we brought the games to a cafeteria at the nearby school to be played by the elementary students, it was a complete disaster.

The kids were bored of the games in a matter of minutes, and actually started begging their teachers to go back to class. I paced around the room trying to coax the children to engage in my students' games, but it was all to no avail. These board games were not interesting to them, and so they would not play. Their boredom in this open space turned to pandemonium, and soon game pieces started flying across the room as the third graders grew more and more restless. Their teachers began yelling at them as the volume in the room rose higher. My students, untrained in how to deal with young kids, started yelling at them as well in their frustration for them to stop ruining their stuff.

Third graders began to cry. Some of my students began to cry.

The principal stomped through the cafeteria doors to ask one of the lead elementary teachers what all of the commotion was, and she immediately turned to me and said that this was not what she expected and asked if we could cut our time short

My students and I felt dejected. A month of hard work they put into creating these games felt wasted, and only served as a distraction for some third graders for about five minutes that morning. Being that we still had fifty minutes left of our planned field trip (remember, we got kicked out of the school), I took them outside to sit in the grass to talk about what just happened.

My sensitive students cried from the feeling of rejection. My emotional students were angry with the grade school kids for not giving their games a chance. Some students were mad at me for not preparing them more for this authentic presentation. And almost all of the students sat on the grass with nothing in their hands, as most of them stuffed their game boards in the trash cans on the way out of the cafeteria (I went back and fished them out later on).

I let it all air out on the lawn next to the elementary school parking lot. When they were done lamenting this experience, I asked them what they have learned so far from it. The first response was, "What do you mean learn from it? This sucks!"

"Yes I agree this was not fun. But what are we learning from it?"

After about a minute of silence, one student suggested that maybe the games we created were not suited for elementary students, and maybe more for high schoolers. Another said that they perhaps should have introduced themselves to the students and "broke the ice" before they started playing the games. I suggested that I probably should have asked the elementary teachers what kind of games their students liked to play with before we started creating games for them.

The tension was releasing in that open space, and only twenty minutes after the event the power of positive failure was starting to have an effect. For the next project in my class, my students created the lesson plans for college students. They were very aware of who their professional audience was, and ensured the products they created were tailored to them. They brought coffee and cookies with them to the presentation to "break the ice" before the lessons. I contacted the professors and asked what their needs were.

My students and I learned from our failure. We did not let it live as a negative experience in the back of our minds the rest of that school year. Instead we embraced and viewed it as an instance where we tried to create something incredible and did not succeed. And that was okay, because this failure shaped us as learners and people, and did more to shape us as characters than an hour of third graders playing board games ever could have.

The key to innovation is vulnerability. Creativity and innovation always involves risk. Risk of failure. Risk of rejection. Risk of judgment. There is a potential for all of these to happen when something new is created.

This leaves the creator vulnerable.

But when vulnerability is embraced, and there is no shame in failure, students have a potential for brilliance, and characters develop into heroes.

"Somewhere, something incredible is waiting to be known."

-Carl Sagan

CHAPTER 10

EPIC

I KNOW A BOY NAMED Drew whose childhood was a living hell. He was placed in foster care because his father committed abuses Drew has never been able to speak of, and his mother became an addict to escape the reminders of those abuses.

Drew is naturally shy, and sat silent at school every day wondering when he would return to his home and stop having to live with someone new every few months. His disposition toward being silent made him a perfect target for bullies, and too many people interpreted his silence as a sign of ineptitude, and wrote him off as a lazy kid who was "too far gone to rescue."

Drew was angry the day I met him on his first day of high school. He wore long sleeves to cover the deep scars on his arms, and glared at me with skeptical eyes when I complimented the coat he was wearing. He took a seat in the back of the classroom, settling in to do what he had been doing for the past seven years of his life: sitting quietly and wondering why no one wanted to be in his family – and why he did not have friends – and what was the point of life if all it ever can be is painful?

He sat there silent.

But Drew was not able to sit quietly for long in my class.

The stories in the projects he was asked to be a part of slowly drew him in. At first he approached them with apathy, and did what was necessary for me and his peers to leave him alone. But as the conflicts that were introduced to his class stirred emotions in his heart, and he realized that he possessed some of the tools to solve these conflicts, Drew began to wake up.

He started speaking up in class and attending workshops. I received emails from him on weekends asking me to clarify questions he had about the projects we were working on. Students started sitting next to him voluntarily, and then Drew made some friends.

The shell that Drew's painful and tragic world had built around him had begun to crack. The truth is, grades were not enough to spur Drew into action, nor was pleasing parents who weren't around or a teacher he did not yet trust. However, the opportunity to be a part of stories that took him on adventures and allowed him to be a hero finally did.

Drew has now graduated high school, and he has not had to wear long sleeves in a long time.

It Works

Drew's story is remarkable and inspiring, but it is not entirely original. I have seen student after student rise from the ashes in the epic classroom. Story-centered, project based, epic learning has created motivated students and helped them realize their own potential. This potential is kept hidden in so many students because of the format of traditional education.

How would Drew ever have learned about his creative ability if all he had ever been allowed to do is sit, remember, and regurgitate? How would Stuart, whose parents told me was a D-student on the brink of having to go to an alternative education program, find out he has a brilliant mind for science as first demonstrated by conquering the Great Pumpkin Drop? How would Emmy, who was a straight-A student her entire life at a traditional school, also discover her penchant for leadership if she could not refine and use it every day in a collaborative classroom?

Following the format of epic learning gives students daily experience using 21st century skills, not just preparing them for the "real world," but also immersing them in it. When students are serving refugees, planting gardens, presenting to business people, proposing ideas to better their communities – they are not getting ready for some day in the future, they are present, and participating in society now. This active participation stimulates excitement and engagement, thus stimulating learning and growth.

It is this motivation that activates academic success in the classroom. Research shows that project based learning increases knowledge retention and decreases high school dropout rates. Students from project based programs score significantly higher on standardized tests like the ACT and SAT. Those same students are attending college at higher rates and completing their degrees in shorter amounts of time.

When project based learning is conducted in the framework of story, and students become characters, and classrooms become settings- the learning becomes permanent. Through the power of story, students make their way across a story arch and experience transformation. Lasting, beneficial change that comes from experiencing the Hero's Journey.

But epic learning does not exist just for students. It exists for teachers as well.

I'll be frank, teaching in an epic classroom is fun. Getting to lead students of any age through an epic tale, and creating an environment where students learn how capable they are to solve problems, is way more interesting to me than just delivering a set of standards and content knowledge.

I still love the academic content that I teach, and will get more than a little enthusiastic when talking about history or literature, but I do not let the content be the center of my classroom. Instead the story is, and it is within this structure that students can learn to fall in love with the content as well.

I love getting to dream up these stories. And I love working with professionals outside of my classroom to work with my kids. And I love bouncing around my classroom helping kids brainstorm and create amazing products to share with others. And I love when kids tell me they didn't sleep at all over the weekend because they were too consumed with creating a project for my class. And I love seeing kids like Drew defy odds as they become immersed in a story that they are the heroes of.

Epic learning does not always have to be huge. Sometimes big is best, and creating projects for students that attract news stations and peak with dramatic climaxes create engaged students and lasting memories. And sometimes, the story can be subtle, and the conflict they must resolve is not life or death, and may not even leave the walls of the classroom. It can be a challenge given by a teacher. Or the search to answer a curiosity a student has. Or even the quest to understand a new concept.

Regardless what the task may be, it should be crafted into a story, an ancient practice that has moved traditions, beliefs, and knowledge across millennia. Stories move people to action. They shape our brains in a physical and permanent way. They provide order in chaos, entertainment in boredom, and transform experiences into lasting learning.

Now *you* get to become a storyteller. Not just a person standing in front of your students, but someone who moves beside them as you embark on adventures. Crafting content into narratives; make your curriculum into a plot. Introducing your students to conflict, and creating an environment, a setting, where heroes can solve it.

You are a teacher. A facilitator.

A *guide.*

And the kids who walk through the halls of your school and sit in desks in your classroom are not numbers the state can keep track of or even just students on your roster. They are characters; brilliant, dynamic, and unique- waiting to embark on the hero's journey.

Characters worthy of a classroom experience that is *epic*.

End Notes

The following are all of the citations throughout the entire book.

---

[1] Stephens GJ, Silbert LJ, Hasson U. Speaker–listener neural coupling underlies successful communication. *Proceedings of the National Academy of Sciences of the United States of America.* 2010;107(32):14425-14430. doi:10.1073/pnas.1008662107.

Also note:
Monarth, H. (2015, December 10). The Irresistible Power of Storytelling as a Strategic Business Tool. Retrieved June 19, 2017, from https://hbr.org/2014/03/the-irresistible-power-of-storytelling-as-a-strategic-business-tool

[2] United States Department of Labor: Bureau of Labor Statistics. (2017, January). Retrieved from https://data.bls.gov/timeseries/CES3000000001

[3] Robinson, K. (2013, May). Transcript of "How to escape education's death valley". Retrieved January 19, 2017, from https://www.ted.com/talks/ken_robinson_how_to_escape_education_s_death_valley/transcript?language=en

[4] Campbell, J. (2008). *The hero with a thousand faces.* Novato, CA: New World Library.

[5] Rowling, JK (2006). "Biography". JKRowling.com. Archived from the original on 21 April 2006. Retrieved 21 May 2006.

[6] This structure is described in page 150 of:
Snyder, B. (2005). *Save the cat!: The last book on screenwriting that youll ever need*. Studio City, CA: Michael Wiese Productions.

[7] Kamenetz, A., & Turner, C. (2016, October 17). The High School Graduation Rate Reaches A Record High - Again. Retrieved June 19, 2017, from
http://www.npr.org/sections/ed/2016/10/17/498246451/the-high-school-graduation-reaches-a-record-high-again

[8] Pressfield, S. (2012). *The war of art: break through the blocks and win your inner creative battles*. New York: Black Irish Entertainment. Page 46.

[9] Quotes. (n.d.). Retrieved June 19, 2017, from
http://www.imdb.com/title/tt0097351/quotes

[10] Note that *Field of Dreams* was actually based upon the following book by W.P. Kinsella:
Kinsella, W. P. (2013). *Shoeless Joe*. London: Friday Project.

[11] Ep. 3: Joseph Campbell and the Power of Myth -- 'The First Storytellers' (1988, June 23). Retrieved June 19, 2017, from

http://billmoyers.com/content/ep-3-joseph-campbell-and-the-power-of-myth-the-first-storytellers-audio/

[12] D. H. Andrews, T. D. Hull and K. DeMeester (eds.), Storytelling as an Instructional Method: Research Perspectives, 3–10. © 2010 Sense Publishers. All Rights Reserved.

[13] Lodge, Sally (18 Jan 2007). "Chooseco Embarks on Its Own Adventure." *Publishers Weekly*. Archived from the original on 2007-10-09. Retrieved 2008-07-10.

[14] Golgowski, N. (2016, June 09). Mike Rowe Tells Grads Not To Follow Their Passion. *The Huffington Post*. Retrieved June 19, 2017, from http://www.huffingtonpost.com/entry/mike-rowe-gives-grad-advice_us_57597c03e4b0e39a28acb092

[15] Johnstone, A. H.; Percival, F. Attention Breaks in Lectures. *Education in Chemistry*, 13, 2, 49-50, Mar 76

[16] Dator, J. (2016, June 22). 1.3 million people are in Cleveland for the parade. SB Nation. Retrieved June 19, 2017, from https://www.sbnation.com/2016/6/22/12005550/cavaliers-parade-cleveland-attendance-1-million

[17] Heath, R. (2010). *Celebrating failure: the power of taking risks, making mistakes, and thinking big.* Petaling Jaya: Advantage Quest Publications.

BRING TREVOR MUIR TO YOUR SCHOOL OR EVENT

Trevor's first passion is exciting students to become enthusiastic, engaged, and impassioned learners. His second love is inspiring others to do the same. Using storytelling, giving examples from the classroom, and sharing proven and effective practices.

Trevor inspires educators to lead a more compelling and engaging classroom. In the past few years, Trevor has given keynotes and workshops to a variety of educators across the country, including a TED Talk at TEDx San Antonio. Trevor offers the perspective of an author, spoken word poet, project based learning expert, and most importantly- a classroom teacher, to help teachers transform their classrooms and communities to reimagine their schools.

What people are saying
about Trevor Muir

"Trevor works hard and is dedicated. He brought so much energy and excitement to our stage!"

-Chris Sandovol
Chair of Programming for TEDx San Antonio

"As a talented education professional, Trevor brings his dynamic, energetic personality to all that he does. His thoughtfulness, concern and compassion for his students is matched with his broad subject matter knowledge and ability to engage others. Trevor represents the excellence of spirit and dedication to the teaching profession that is often hard to come by."

-Ron Houtman
Ed Tech Consultant, Director of REMC8, MACUL
Board Member

"Trevor's keynote was inspiring. His presentations really challenged us to rethink our planning and preparation."

-Dan Diedrich
Founder of Horizons Community High School

Keynote and Workshop Descriptions

The Epic Classroom: Is there any point in learning something if you're just going to forget it? (Keynote and Workshop)

And this begs a bigger question: if learning is not memorable, should it even be considered learning? Trevor Muir shares how educators can shape their classrooms using the power of storytelling and brain science to achieve real student engagement, and in return, learning that is permanent and memorable. Any teacher, in any subject area, and in any grade level can use these practical and proven practices to transform their classrooms into settings where students are engaged, challenged, and transformed.

Superhero Mountain Climbers and How to Make Learning Authentic (Keynote)

A student's potential for success is often measured using grades, and quite often this measure misses the whole picture of who a student is and what they are capable of. Trevor destroys the dominant myth that grades are the primary indicator of a student's success, and shares stories, research, and practices that reveal how authentic learning can give any student the opportunity to grow, strengthen, and thrive---oh, and get good grades.

Story-Centric Learning (Workshop)

Storytelling is essential to the human experience. This medium of communication is not only proven to be the best way of sharing information, but also for learning and retaining that information. Class can be designed and taught in the format of a story. This workshop gives concrete methods, practices, and resources to create a story-centric classroom, an innovative project based learning model.

Project Based Learning 101 (Workshop)

Trevor's PBL 101 course was developed after years of working in a New Tech project based learning school, as well as his experience as a Buck Institute National Faculty member. Through this engaging and learning-intensive program, Trevor teaches any educator from any grade level how to implement project based learning in their school and classroom.

Using Technology to Create Authentic Learning (Workshop)

There is a difference between getting students ready for the real world and actually immersing them in it. Making learning real and authentic breeds enthusiasm in the classroom, and enthusiasm breeds success. This session will be a conversation of how certain technologies can be used to enhance authenticity in the classroom.

Speaking Inquiries:

Email Trevor at trevor@trevormuir.com to have him speak at your school, district, or organization.

ABOUT THE AUTHOR

Trevor is an author, speaker, storyteller, and above all else- a teacher. After working in an extremely innovative project based learning school, and then in a very traditional high school, Trevor has learned that no matter what environment or technologies a school has, the story being told in classrooms is what's most important.

He first shared this message at TEDx San Antonio, and has since traveled around the country sharing the value of epic learning with educators. His work has been featured in the *Huffington Post*, *WeAreTeachers*, and *The Creative Classroom*.

Trevor's popular Facebook page, The Epic Classroom, regularly shares informational and inspiring videos.

Trevor lives in Grand Rapids, Michigan, with his wife and two children.

Contact Trevor:

Email: trevor@trevormuir.com
Website: trevormuir.com
Facebook: The Epic Classroom
YouTube: Trevor Muir
Twitter: @trevormuir

CPSIA information can be obtained
at www.ICGtesting.com
Printed in the USA
LVHW112159080519
617192LV00001B/257/P